PRO SECRETS OF HEAVY ROCK SINGING

Ron Keel biography courtesy of www.ironhorseband.com

Printed in the UK by MPG Books, Bodmin

Published by: Sanctuary Publishing Limited, 45-53 Sinclair Road,
London W14 ONS, United Kingdom

www.sanctuarypublishing.com

Copyright: Bill Martin, 2002

Cover photo © Getty/PhotoDisc/Lawrence Lawry

ISBN: 1-86074-437-0

PRO SECRETS OF HEAVY ROCK SINGING

Bill Martin

Sanctuary

contents

introduction

People have asked me, 'Why a book about heavy rock singing?' The truth is, I've always loved the power and energy of heavy music. There is something invigorating about the sound of a guitar running through a distortion box, backed by throbbing bass and pounding drums. I came of age in the '70s and '80s, when classic rock, power metal and glam metal dominated the airwaves. Many of these bands had lead singers who could do some amazing things with their voice. Throughout the '90s and into this century, more great singers emerged, many of them with strong, deep, baritone voices that were quite different from the singers of decades prior. Although heavy rock continues to evolve, one thing has always remained constant: it is arguably the most challenging and vocally taxing genre of music to sing. I have often wondered, 'How do these rock singers sing so hard and so heavy for years without destroying their voices?'

There are several good singing books on the market (see the Appendix at the back of this book for ones I recommend), but all of them are written by singing teachers. I couldn't find all the answers I wanted in these books. I wanted to know how heavy rock singers produced the rasp and rough edge in their voices. How do they keep their voices strong while on the road? What do they drink and eat? How do they warm up before a show? Have they ever taken vocal lessons? How do they hit high notes? I wanted to know a lot of things! Eventually, I realised that if I wanted to know how pro rock singers mastered their craft, I was going to have to ask them myself. That's what I did.

The fact that there are so many interviews in this book is a tribute to the passion that these singers feel for singing. I had no agent, no publicist, no journalistic affiliations and no music contacts whatsoever when I sought these interviews. Nevertheless, these singers responded eagerly and shared their tricks, secrets and habits – some good, some bad – candidly.

While I have enjoyed singing in my life, I realised early on that I was not naturally gifted but that, through hard work, I could become pretty good. I believe this is the case for most people. Not everyone can be a great singer, but almost anyone can be pretty good if they work hard enough. While this book focuses on singing, it also holds fascinating insights for anyone interested in a behind-the-scenes look at what it takes to perform at a professional level in a band. It's intended for all music fans and musicians, regardless of what kind of music they enjoy or what instruments they play. My hope for this book is that it becomes an inspiration for you when you need motivation. I also hope that the secrets in these pages help you to establish good vocal habits so that you can sing the way you want to for many years to come. Rock on!

chapter 1

getting to know your voice

Any singer serious about his or her profession should have a good idea about what voice type he or she has. Knowing your voice type is extremely helpful when it comes to picking suitable songs to sing. There's an irony, though, in that singers often believe that the grass is greener on the other side: high-singing tenors wish they had a richer bottom end, while warm-toned baritones wish they could hit the higher notes. But no particular voice type is 'better' than another, and you can be successful with any voice type. Use your strengths to get the most out of your voice: if you're a baritone such as Jim Morrison, don't force yourself to sing Journey songs; if you have a high voice, in the Freddie Mercury range, lay off the Barry White.

Voice types are defined by both range and timbre (tonal quality). The five main voice types are listed below, along with examples of each style

female voices

- **Soprano** - This is the highest female voice type.
- **Coloratura Soprano** - This is the very high, light, floating voice such as that of Mariah Carey and Celine Dion.
- **Mezzo-Soprano** - Exponents of this type of singing have a slightly lower range, such as Joan Jett, Jewel and Lita Ford.
- **Contralto** - The lowest female voice; has a darker tone than a soprano with a fuller bottom end. Toni Braxton fits into this category.

male voices

- **Tenor** - The highest male voice.
- **Lyric Tenor** - Light, floating voice. Best suited to soaring, clean vocal lines. Think Ian Gillan, Steve Perry, Sting and Robert Plant.
- **Dramatic Tenor** - Similar range to a lyric tenor but with darker, fuller low notes. More suited to rough singing.

Most of the singers interviewed in this book are tenors. A classic metal lyric tenor is Geoff Tate, while a prototypical metal dramatic tenor is Bruce Dickinson. Both singers have that tenor range, but the tonal qualities of their voices are extremely different. Bruce Dickinson is a very loud and heavy-toned singer, while Geoff Tate has lighter overtones.

- **Baritone** - Baritones have more bottom end than a tenor, but less full-voice high end. Jim Morrison, James Hetfield, Matt Barlow, Danzig, Elvis Presley, Scott Stapp and Aaron Lewis are all baritones. Baritones can also be lyric or dramatic in tone.
- **Bass** - The lowest male voice and not particularly common in heavy rock music.

voice range classifications

The following chart shows the common ranges of the five basic voice types, represented by the notes of a piano. C1 is the first C on the piano, E8 the last E. The letter represents the note and the number represents the octave. For example, C4, commonly called 'middle C', is the C note that begins the fourth octave on the piano.

The dark-shaded area shows the range of the singer's full voice. The lighter-shaded area shows the falsetto range for men. For a coloratura soprano, this area indicates the whistle register. The black square with white lettering on the chart indicates the lowest comfortable note in the range. The white squares indicate the 'break notes' between registers.

| C1 | D1 | E1 | F1 | G1 | A1 | B1 | C2 | D2 | E2 | F2 | **G2** | A2 | B2 | C3 | D3 | E3 | F3 | G3 | A3 | B3 | C4 | D4 | E4 | F4 | G4 | A4 | B5 | C5 | D5 | E5 | F5 | G5 | A5 |

Bass

| G1 | A1 | B1 | C2 | D2 | E2 | F2 | G2 | **A2** | B2 | C3 | D3 | E3 | F3 | G3 | A3 | B3 | C4 | D4 | E4 | F4 | G4 | A4 | B4 | C5 | D5 | E5 | F5 | G5 | A5 | B5 | C6 | D6 | E6 |

Baritone

| B1 | C2 | D2 | E2 | F2 | G2 | A2 | B2 | **C3** | D3 | E3 | F3 | G3 | A3 | B3 | C4 | D4 | E4 | F4 | G4 | A4 | B4 | C5 | D5 | E5 | F5 | G5 | A5 | B5 | C6 | D6 | E6 | F6 | G6 |

Tenor

| F2 | G2 | A2 | B2 | C3 | D3 | E3 | F3 | **G3** | A3 | B3 | C4 | D4 | E4 | F4 | G4 | A4 | B4 | C5 | D5 | E5 | F5 | G5 | A5 | B5 | C6 | D6 | E6 | F6 | G6 | A6 | B6 | C7 | D7 |

Contralto

| A2 | B2 | C3 | D3 | E3 | F3 | G3 | **A3** | B3 | C4 | D4 | E4 | F4 | G4 | A4 | B4 | C5 | D5 | E5 | F5 | G5 | A5 | B5 | C6 | D6 | E6 | F6 | G6 | A6 | B6 | C7 | D7 | E7 | F7 |

Mezzo-soprano

| B2 | C3 | D3 | E3 | F3 | G3 | A3 | B3 | **C4** | D4 | E4 | F4 | G4 | A4 | B4 | C5 | D5 | E5 | F5 | G5 | A5 | B5 | C6 | D6 | E6 | F6 | G6 | A6 | B6 | C7 | D7 | E7 | F7 | G7 |

Coloratura soprano

Used by permission and adapted from a chart © Eric Armstrong of Roosevelt University

voice registers

So, what is a break note? It's simply a note that falls on the pitch between registers. All voices experience register changes, or breaks, which are transition points in the voice where the tonal quality changes. It's like the point in a car engine where the gears shift. It often sounds like a crack in an inexperienced singer's voice, but it can be smoothed over with practice.

There is much debate on whether the voice actually has different registers, and whether or not it is helpful to think of the voice as having breaks and registers. Some voice coaches teach a theory of 'one voice', with no breaks. Nevertheless, there appear to be distinct changes in vocal quality that occur in almost all voices at specific notes in the range. For that reason, and because many of the singers in this book speak in terms of registers, we'll have a look at them. They are generally called *chest voice*, *head voice* and *falsetto*.

Chest voice is the lower part of the range before the break into head voice at around E or F above middle C. These low notes buzz or hum primarily in the chest and include your normal speaking pitch.

The head register, above the break note, is where some of the bottom end leaves the voice; it's still a full voice capable of much power. This is found in much heavy rock singing because head voice tends to carry well over heavy music. Historically, heavy metal has involved loud, overdriven guitars and soaring vocals – good examples of this type of music include such bands as Led Zeppelin, Black Sabbath, Deep Purple, Judas Priest and Iron Maiden. In recent years, the predominant use of chest voice has become popular, too.

You'll notice from the chart that each voice type has two breaks at approximately E and an octave apart. The first break doesn't usually present major problems for a rock singer; it simply separates the very low chest voice from the middle-chest voice. The second break is more prominent and triggers the transition from chest voice to head voice.

Notice how the register changes occur at pretty much the same places for both men and women of all voice types. However, there is some minor fluctuation from person to person in the exact location of register change. For example, some basses change to head voice at D or D♯ instead of E; some tenors change at F or F♯ instead of E.

Further up the scale (denoted by the lighter grey squares in the chart), the male voice breaks into falsetto, which is actually a false voice with very few overtones. Falsetto is produced when the vocal cords are kept apart and air blows freely through them relatively unimpeded. In chest and head voice, the cords are pressed close together, releasing small, concentrated puffs of air. Some tenors do not have a discernible break between head voice and falsetto. They can carry a rich, full tone all the way to the top of their range.

Among female singers, coloratura sopranos sometimes have register above head voice called the *whistle register*. You can hear it used by female pop singers including Mariah Carey and Christina Aguilera.

Using a keyboard and the chart in this chapter, you can see where chest voice changes into head voice and head voice changes into falsetto. You should be able to feel and hear the changes. If the chest-to-head break is a problem area for you, try singing scales through the break. This will help you carry the thickness of chest voice into the head voice and smoothe out the break. You can do the same thing to carry head voice over the falsetto break.

Try to get a feel for the type of song which seems easy for you to sing. You might find that you have a lyric voice that has difficulty growling or singing short, choppy phrases. You might sound great singing high songs with long, melodic lines, or high, raspy singing might be easy for you. On the other hand, low-chest-voice growling might be your particular strength. Wherever your voice stands out, you can capitalise on your strengths by singing and writing songs in that style.

chapter 2

breath control

Breath control is probably the most important skill for a novice singer to learn: it's the foundation of good singing. When breathing for singing, your shoulders should not rise at all, except at the end of a very deep breath. Your stomach should extend naturally, as if you're pulling the air down your throat and directly into your stomach. Your lower back will also expand. This is called *diaphragmatic breathing*, meaning that you're allowing your diaphragm to extend.

> *'Doing a lot of breathing exercises has been a critical part of why I can still sing'*
>
> – Kip Winger

When your stomach doesn't move but your chest and shoulders rise, you're taking shallow breaths and limiting the extension of the diaphragm. You'll notice that the more your chest rises when you breathe, the tighter your throat gets. The throat closes to resist the air pressure. The support muscles in the abdomen, ribs and back are being under-used while the throat over-compensates. If you sing like this, you'll find yourself out of the band. When you notice it, correct it immediately, not by sucking in more air, but by exhaling everything from your chest until you have nothing left, then inhale naturally, with the stomach and lower back expanding.

Contrary to what many people think, breath support does not involve tightening the upper abdominal muscles, as when doing sit-ups. The abs might flex, but it is a complementary reaction to the tightening of other muscles. When the diaphragm expands, the organs in the abdomen bulge out to make room for the lungs to expand. The abdominal wall extends and hardens in response. The rib cage pushes down and out while the low abs push up so that the air is pressurised and held between the two, as if you held a balloon firmly between your two hands. At the same time, there should be little to no tension in the throat.

All of this muscle activity should occur simultaneously with the initiation of the note. If you tighten up all your muscles before you hear any sound, your voice will not be free. Think of breath support as a system of muscles working in coordination. If you push too hard in any one area, you'll throw off the whole system.

On a very high or heavy note, proper breath support can involve a prominent pressing down or bracing sensation. The lower back muscles tighten. The intercostal muscles (the muscles between the ribs) remain flexed to prevent the collapse of the rib cage. The lower abs below the navel will tuck in and tighten, becoming a sort of shelf that supports the air.

Proper breath control involves more than just diaphragm and abdominal strength. The vocal cords must be able to resist the air pressure. The intercostal, abdominal and back muscles must all work together to ensure that the air is released in a controlled way. If the ribs collapse too quickly, you'll over-blow your vocal cords and feel winded. The larynx is like a pressure valve in that it ultimately decides whether or not air is released.

Controlled air-release exercises are good ways to strengthen and warm up the breath-support system. Take a deep diaphragmatic breath (your stomach should extend, your shoulders should rise only at the very end of the deep breath), put your tongue on the roof of your mouth and go 'ssssssss' like the sound of an air hose – make this sound as loudly as you can. You'll notice that your lower abs (below the naval) will tighten and also that your rib cage will brace out and down. This is the same sensation you should feel on very high head-voice notes and is the same mechanism you'll experience on all notes, but it will be subtle on easier notes, so you won't really notice it as much.

Posture is also important. You can't be slumped over because your diaphragm won't have room to extend. You'll notice that most sitting singers have a straight posture. You can try this yourself: slump over and try to hit a note (it will sound anywhere from decent to horrible), then hit the same note with the same effort while sitting up straight. You'll notice better resonance and a fuller tone. The note will feel free and more controllable. This is the difference that posture makes.

the pros speak

JAMES LABRIE (DREAM THEATER): 'If you're using your diaphragm properly, your stomach comes out. You try to imagine a big rubber tyre in your abdominal area and you fill up your air there. Then you would take that and blow the air out of your mouth in a very controlled way. All you could do was just bend the flame on the candle. You would never blow it out. You would see how long you could bend that flame without running out of air. And the key was that you would go for as long as you could. So it would be ten seconds when you first started. Then you'd get up to 30 seconds, then a minute. It's all showing you that, if you breathe properly and you develop your diaphragm, you have unlimited amounts of air.'

GEOFF TATE (QUEENSRŸCHE): 'When you're first learning, I think breathing technique is incredibly important to master. It's definitely what saves you in the endurance area of singing. It's what makes it so you can sing those two-hour shows. It's like any instrument – you've got to practise it to get good. I think so many people get frustrated and give up. Or they learn how to do it in a different way that doesn't require so much discipline.'

GEOFF TATE (ON THE SENSATION OF BREATH SUPPORT): 'It's like doing squats in the gym – it's very similar to that kind of sensation. In fact, you'll notice that really good singers don't have the six-pack abs. You can't develop those particular ab muscles extensively if you're a singer because it reduces your diaphragm abilities. Most singers are more barrel-chested.'

DAVID DRAIMAN (DISTURBED): 'Anybody that tells you "Sing from your diaphragm" is lying to you because the diaphragm is not a muscle that is under conscious control. It's an unconscious muscle; it's not meant to be used consciously. That is the mistake most people make when they try to figure out where their power is supposed to come from when singing this type of music. You have muscles that help with your breathing that are around your lower to middle back. Those are the muscles that should be used for advanced technique and additional power in this type of singing. Your ribs should expand, giving your lungs more capacity, and your diaphragm should be completely relaxed. The muscles that you're using are your breathing muscles in your low to mid back.'

CHUCK BILLY (TESTAMENT): 'A major part of my singing is having a lot of wind, so I do a lot of running and bicycling, just building up my lungs, because without that I can't pull it off. So when I'm on the road, I do a lot of holding my breath. I just hold it for like two and a half, three minutes. Just close your eyes and hold it; go into another world.

JOE LYNN TURNER (RAINBOW, DEEP PURPLE, YNGWIE MALMSTEEN): 'Most people think they have to take big breaths, but it's not about big breaths. It's really about holding the air inside the solar plexus. This is why a lot of big singers have barrel chests, because of this muscle development. For a small guy, I have this huge chest because of these muscles in the solar plexus area.'

GROG PREBBLE (DIE SO FLUID): 'I had a handful of singing lessons when I was about 16 which taught me how to breathe correctly. It's lucky really because I wouldn't have bothered to find out otherwise. It set me in good stead, even if lying on the floor with phone directories on my stomach seemed bizarre at the time. I learned how to breathe properly by expanding the diaphragm and pushing out the stomach as I breathed in.'

BRUCE HALL (ORDER OF THE ILLUMINATI, AGENT STEEL): 'When I first started, I would breathe like I was singing all the time, right up until the last breath I took before going to sleep. It trained me into always breathing this way, always from the diaphragm. If you watch me talk to you, you'll never see my shoulders go up.'

COREY BROWN (MAGNITUDE 9): 'The first thing I learned to develop, when I was 14, was learning to take a breath without raising my shoulders. I'd fold a piece of paper in half and stand it up across the table from me, and I would practise taking a deep breath and trying to blow it over. So if I blew it over at two feet, I would slide it back another foot and so on until I couldn't blow it over any more. I do exercises when I'm sitting around: I'll take a deep breath and count out loud as far as I can before I run out of breath. That's a good exercise for the diaphragm. When I first started singing I used to lay on my back and put a couple books on my stomach and try to inhale and raise the books, then exhale and watch the books fall.'

building breath control

One way to look at breath support is to mimic the breathing of a baby. Babies are masterful breathers. Volume is all about breath control. Look at how loud a baby can scream. A baby's vocal cords are thin, tiny little things. Its lungs are no bigger than your fist. Yet it can wail. It's because of good breath support. A baby's stomach expands when he or she breathes. Babies are sort of barrel-chested because of their strong breath-support muscle development.

Good breath control is maintained by being aware of sensations that are wrong. We are all human and our breathing is affected by anxiety and stress, which will make you either breathe shallow and high or hold your breath unconsciously. So you have to be aware of things not feeling right: you're not getting enough power, you're losing control, your throat feels tense, you feel winded. These are the clues that you must be sensitive to:

they mean it's time to check your breathing. If you're new to singing, you might feel out of breath a lot. You might yawn or belch. All of this is natural until you strengthen and coordinate the breathing-support system.

chapter 3

the power equation

Don't let the thought of maths scare you. All you need to remember is this simple formula: resonation + volume = power. What, then, is resonation? Put simply, resonation is an amplification of sound resulting from vibrations in the bone cavities. Depending on the density and size of the bone structure, specific frequencies resonate more than others, creating your unique voice. These resonations add overtones to the voice to round out the overall tone. Resonation is the key to making your notes full and rich.

the resonators

Depending on the pitch you're singing, you'll experience several specific resonating sensations. You'll notice that the higher you go up the scale, the areas that resonate also rise, thus high notes tend to cause vibrations in the head and face. This is because the bones and cavities in the head are smaller than those in the chest. They respond to high frequencies, whereas for something as large as the sternum to resonate, larger sound waves are needed. So the chest resonates most noticeably in low pitches. Chest voice is called such because of the buzz in the chest. Sing a low note with your hand on your chest and you'll feel the vibrations.

The throat is also a major resonator because it is a hollow cavity. It resonates most in the mid-range. A good, strong mid-range note will hum between the larynx and collarbone.

The mouth also serves to amplify and thicken tone. If you're trying to sing cleanly and clearly, filling the mouth with tone is probably the best way to gauge how well you're singing. The mouth tends to resonate more in mid-range notes, but it helps on any pitch to think about filling your mouth with as much tone as possible. Let the tone swirl around in your mouth until you feel as if you could physically bite down on it.

Another major resonator is the 'mask'. The mask is the triangular area from the bridge of the nose down to the corners of the mouth. The hard palate, or the roof of the mouth, is also part of it. Mask resonation is what is meant when vocal coaches say, 'Place the note forward.' The mask adds brightness to the tone and provides carrying power. If your notes are too throaty, they need to be placed more in the mask. One way to do this is to simply imagine the note shooting like an arrow out of your mouth through the fleshy spot right behind your top front teeth where the hard palate begins. Free up your throat muscles and your tongue, allowing the note to come out unimpeded.

When going through a register break, put the same feeling in that fleshy part behind your top teeth. This closes the note and keeps it under control until those tricky break notes are passed.

Another resonator, the nose, can buzz on high notes and on any note that is placed there. Even low notes can be made to sound nasal. Adding a slight nasal buzz on low notes adds brightness, which is helpful if your low notes are too muddy. Nevertheless, you don't want to jam the sound completely into your nose because it will then lose its bottom end and become less flexible.

Resonators can all be manipulated to your advantage. For instance, if you want to sing a mid-range note that sounds dark and scary, look for that chest buzz to add depth to it. If you want to have fuller high notes, allow for more hum in your throat. Anchor the tone there. The key is to learn the nuances of your voice so that you can make adjustments when necessary. If you tend to sound shrill at certain pitches, notice what happens in your resonation. The tone probably falls too far forward in the mask or bangs excessively off the hard palate. The correction is to open the back of your mouth and allow the note to hum there and in the throat. This balances out the note's tendency to fall forward.

the pros speak

RALF SCHEEPERS (PRIMAL FEAR): I can really feel a good resonance in the hard palate when I'm singing low tones and A, E, O and I vowels. The resonance is in the torso as well, but not as strong as in the palate and the mask of my head. When I scream those high notes, I can feel it very hard in the bones of the head.

RAY ALDER (FATES WARNING): I feel it behind my eyes. When I was taking lessons with Mary Burns, she was saying, 'Do you feel this here? Where's this note? Where's that note?' Finally, I realised that my high notes are behind my eyes. It's the weirdest thing.

GEOFF TATE (QUEENSRŸCHE): It's almost like you don't have to hear it; you can feel what the note is. For me, it's more like I can tell if I'm singing on pitch or if I'm a little off by the way it feels. Most of the time, I don't think about that kind of stuff. I just do it. That's because I'm used to my programmes. In the early days, I remember thinking, 'Okay, where's my diaphragm in relation to my throat right now?' and 'How's the note feel in the top of my head?' That's where I always feel it: in the top of my head.

JOE LYNN TURNER (RAINBOW, DEEP PURPLE): In the studio I have to take Advils before I sing because I'll definitely get a headache – there's no question about it. I will sing so hard and so high, and with such passion, that I will be straining my whole body. It's kind of like lifting weights: you're gonna feel it afterwards.

JOE COMEAU (ANNIHILATOR): You don't have to rip your throat out, but you have to reach a certain level where you're singing with conviction. It's not an insanely high volume, but just at a consist volume that's pretty loud. I've found that the better vocalists do that, because you don't want to use too much compression. You want a consistent volume.

MATT BARLOW (ICED EARTH): Opera is more geared toward stage performance without any kind of miking. It's a totally different animal. From what I have done in theatre, it's all about projection. And rock 'n' roll is more about doing different things with your voice at lower volumes. Not that operatic singing is without dynamics, but it's not like rock 'n' roll.

power

Resonation is certainly more noticeable at loud volumes. But volume does not translate to better resonance. In fact, volume is overrated in this respect. More important is the carrying power of the voice. That is, can the voice cut through the music and sound 'up front'? This all depends on resonation. Often, when we sing loudly we throw our voices off balance, losing resonance because we're pushing too hard. The voice feels and sounds smaller, so we compensate by singing even more loudly. Soon enough, you end up losing your voice.

The way to achieve power in your voice is to allow its natural resonation. You shouldn't have to sing at full volume all of the time – even in heavy rock music. This will just burn you out. Singers who have to scream all the time often wear out quickly on tour. Many great singers, such as Ronnie James Dio and Geoff Tate, are able to sound great at a medium volume, only slightly above a conversational volume.

The important thing is to learn to use resonance to enhance tone. A powerful sound comes from a combination of volume and good resonance. The resonance must be present even on quiet notes. From there, you can gradually get louder and louder while maintaining the same areas of resonation. For example, sing a mid-range scale at a volume just above a whisper. Feel the resonation in your throat, mask and chest. Slowly increase volume without losing those sensations. You'll notice that you sound louder even though you aren't 'maxed out' on volume.

Because resonance is a natural result of relaxed singing, the impediments to good resonation all result from a misuse of the singing muscles. For example, if you tighten your throat too much, you tend to lose balance. A tight throat tends to absorb sound, whereas relaxed throat muscles reflect and enhance tone. Also, if your tongue is pushing the larynx down, you lose flexibility and ring. If your stomach is tense, your throat closes up. If you're tired or slouched over, your diaphragm won't support you correctly, and it'll feel like you're singing with a sock in your mouth. Remember: good resonation is a natural result of unforced singing.

warming up

As with any activity that involves the use of muscles, warming up is vital to a long and healthy singing career. Power-singing without warm-up exercises is like doing weight-lifting without stretching first: you're asking for trouble. Just as you can pull a muscle weight-lifting, you can pull a singing muscle in the larynx and neck if you don't warm up. You'll also find that it'll help you sing for longer periods of time with more control and less wear and tear. Consequently, your singing ability will improve faster.

Singing requires coordination between the abs, diaphragm and vocal muscles. When your abs and diaphragm aren't warmed up, they don't regulate the airflow properly, tending to allow either too much or too little air to the vocal cords. Even if they do allow the right amount of air to the cords, the vocal cords and muscles of the larynx must also be warmed up so that they can withstand that pressure, or they'll blow open. Your singing voice will lack control and power, resulting in a tendency to use more throat tension, which wears out your vocal cords.

Even seasoned professionals don't start ripping into the high notes without thorough preparation and a session of warm-up exercises first. Most pros start with phrases in the lower registers. Similarly, it's not good to start out at full volume. Treat your voice with care and respect, starting at a conversation-style pitch and volume. Only then should you ease into loud, high singing.

The following exercises mentioned by the pros are elaborated on in the next chapter. Some singers simply warm up to songs in their set, which needs no further elaboration. Warming up this way is fine as long as you ease your way into the difficult phrases. Whatever you do to warm up, don't put difficult songs among the first three songs that you sing. Save the songs with really high notes or difficult growling for later on in the set.

You'll notice that everyone seems to have his or her own way of warming up. All of this variation among great singers should serve as a source of comfort, proving that there is no single 'right' way to get ready to sing. Some singers do impromptu scales, while others adhere to a strict pattern of vocal exercises. Some do siren-like warm-ups: one continuous note going up and down; some just sing songs and ignore scales; others hum scales, and so on.

The length and timing of warm-up exercises can also vary. Some singers warm up for an hour (probably too long), while others warm up for five minutes or so. It's common for singers to start warming up about 30 minutes or so before show-time, although some singers warm up an hour or more prior to going on-stage.

Despite all of these differences, one practice is common: most singers start low in their range and work their way up to the high notes. Geoff Tate is the only singer interviewed here who said that he starts in head voice and works his way gradually down. This probably works for him because he is a tenor who does most of his singing in head voice. The general principle is to start in a comfortable area and save the hard parts until your voice is warm. The pros highlight this and other key points next.

the pros speak

GEOFF TATE (QUEENSRŸCHE): 'I sort of warm up all day long, really. I warm up in the morning just by singing to myself, kind of using the head voice mostly, just opening up that top end of my voice early on in the day. Then, as the day goes on, I kind of work into the lower registers. By show-time I'm very warmed up and ready. I sing the latest material I'm working on, or I sing classical scales, because I'm really into classical music as a sort of disciplinary music to listen to.'

DAVID DRAIMAN (DISTURBED): 'The most important part of any warm-up a singer does prior to singing is actually relaxing themselves, making sure that all the parts of their body are loose. I'll go through scales, and depending on where I happen to have a little bit of difficulty on the scale, that is the area that I concentrate on.'

BRUCE DICKINSON (IRON MAIDEN): 'When I'm warming up, I like to produce my head voice with my mouth closed and my teeth together. I've got this sort of manic grin on my face and I try to shake my teeth loose — the front teeth — until the whole front of my face is vibrating. When I can do that fairly effortlessly, I join up the other two spaces. I will take a note — not singing necessarily loudly — and just hold it and vibrate, internally, this little space in my head. I'll move it around so that the front of my nose, the back of my nose, my teeth and everything are humming like tuning forks. I try to keep that note as long as I possibly, possibly, *possibly* can without any tension in my throat muscles.'

JAMES LABRIE (DREAM THEATER): 'I do cleft scales, like 'Ah-ah-ah-ah-ahhhh [five-note ascending scale]'. You obviously start at your very low register notes and you build yourself up gradually. You can take little breaks, have a drink of water, walk around, stretch. Then, when you come back from a break, you go into your higher notes. But you never ever take yourself to your peak – your highest, highest notes. Let the body warm up gradually.'

RIK EMMETT (TRIUMPH): 'I generally simply make up melodies in either the Dorian or Aeolian mode and improvise little Celtic folk melodies using nonsense vowel sounds.'

CHUCK BILLY (TESTAMENT): 'I do a lot of humming, deep, deep humming where the voice vibrates. Once you get that sensation like your nose starts tickling, you know it's starting to work. On the road, that's how I gauge it. I've been doing this for so long now that, once my nose starts tickling, I know I'm ready to go.'

RIPPER OWENS (JUDAS PRIEST): 'I don't overdo it; I just make sure it gets warmed up. I won't sing a scale. It's almost just like a sliding scale – I just slide up from my chest voice into a high falsetto. And I'll do it roughly most of the time – I'll just go from low to high. Then I'll start singing a few high notes clean. I just make sure I have my voice, really. I think that's what my warm-ups are for: to make sure I'm not gonna walk on-stage and not be able to hit something.'

RAY ALDER (FATES WARNING): 'I try to find a quiet spot. The best place for me is a bathroom or a room without carpets that has some sort of natural reverb. That's the best because you can hear it in your head. It just feels better; you don't have to push as hard. I go from the lows to the highs, move around a little bit, just try to warm the voice up, do a couple of scales of my own discovery. I just pretty much make them up. I might do a couple of lines in the songs, ones that are particularly hard or something, but my warm-up really only consists of four or five minutes.'

WADE BLACK (SEVEN WITCHES): 'What I usually do is kind of like a hum, kind of like keeping it in my head. And what I'll do is I'll go up and down my entire range. You know, kind of like "Bbbbbbbbbb" with my lips. Humming's good, too, as long as you have a bright, resonating sound in your head.'

JOHN BUSH (ARMORED SAINT): 'I do this new warm-up now that sounds like this: "Ahh-ahhh [sings two notes a fifth apart]". It's a good warm-up. Big intervals. You just go up the scale. And that one will really let you know where you stand as far as warming up goes. To me, the warm-up is just a way to save my voice. If you go out there cold and just start screaming, which I do sometimes, you're just gonna blow it out. It's a way to get your voice to a gradual adjustment.'

JORNE LANDE (ARK): 'I sing parts of what I'm going to sing during the show. I just try a couple of lines or so. Of course, I'm trying first a couple of lower notes to check it. Then I increase a little bit and go up in range and do some of the higher parts. It's to check it – not necessarily for power, just to feel where I'm at.'

TIMO KOTIPELTO (STRATOVARIUS): 'There's one secret that I have: I'm using a pipe that's made of... I think it's kind of a silicon, but it's elastic, and I put it in the water and gargle. Then I do some exercises: I have a glass of water and one end of the pipe is in the water, the other end is in my mouth. Then I make sounds and make the water bubble. What happens is that the water resonates and sends the vibrations back to my vocal cords. This actually works. It's not bullshit. I go to a throat doctor at least once a year just to check out if everything's okay with my vocal cords and she told me that this is a very good treatment. When some of her patients have vocal problems, she tells them that they should use this thing. I'm using this as a warm-up, and you can feel it in your neck. It actually works. I just do some things like 'Whooooooo-oooooo-oooooo [owl-like sounds]'. I start very low and widen the range a little bit. Then I even do some high falsetto notes as well. This is only two or three minutes. This can be two, three or maybe even four hours before the show. I do it every time. Sometimes I even do it if I have problems during the show, like if the vocal cords feel tight or I can't keep the voice completely clean, then I use this method after the show, but only for one minute. After the pipe, I start doing small exercises very softly. If I can easily hit the high notes, I probably warm up only for ten minutes. But sometimes I warm up for 20 or 30 minutes. If I have to sing only one song, if it's a special TV thing or whatever, then I have to warm up more.'

While some singers are not fond of warm-up exercises, every singer interviewed does some kind of vocal preparation before a show, even if it's only five minutes of improvised notes. The amount of time you need for warming up is affected by how often you sing. If you're singing five or more nights a week, your voice is probably in good shape and will need less warming up than if you sing once a week.

where to warm up

When warming up, you'll want to go to a private spot where you won't be distracted. If you tend to get inhibited or show off in front of people, you have another reason to find a private spot.

Some of the pros mention that they prefer to warm up in the bathroom. A typical bathroom has natural reverb that prevents you from singing too hard. The bathroom sound builds confidence because the reverb makes you sound full and powerful. If you can warm up in a bathroom after a hot shower you get the added benefit of warm, moist air, which will soothe your vocal cords, pharynx and windpipe.

If you can't sing in the bathroom, choose another room that has solid, reflective walls. Rooms that dampen sound are not preferred for warm-up exercises. For instance, closets usually have too many soft materials – clothing, boxes, etc – that absorb sound. Likewise, car interiors are usually lined with carpeting. These dampening environments tend to make you sound small, meaning that you'll be tempted to push harder and sing louder. Another problem with singing in the car is road noise – if you have a noisy vehicle, try not to sing there at all.

I find it helpful to warm up on all the vowel sounds scaling up and down the range for at least ten minutes. I do five-note scales ascending then descending on the same breath. To help get the proper buzzing resonance, start the vowels with 'Nnnn' or 'Mmmm'. For example: 'Nnneee, Nnnaaayyy, Niiiii, Nnnooo, Nuuuuu.' After this, I like to sing sections of songs. This helps hone my breathing technique and phrasing. Here, then, are some of the warm-up exercises mentioned by the pros in more detail.

the rattlesnake warm-up

The Rattlesnake warm-up used by Wade Black (Seven Witches), Andy Franck (Brainstorm, Symphorce) and Sean Peck (Cage) uses the tongue and lips to resist the air. Place your tongue on the roof of your mouth and roll the 'Rrrrr' sound, as in 'Rrrricky Rrrricarrrrdo'. Allow your lips to flap simultaneously. You can also do this exercise with just the lips – no tongue.

Try to keep the 'Bbbbrrrrrr' going while you perform scales throughout your range. This protects the cords from excessive air pressure, because the tongue and lips resist most of the air. Start in your low and mid-range notes. Then, after five or ten minutes, move into head voice. If it's a particularly rough day for the voice, spend more time in the lower registers before moving to head voice. The key to this warm-up is keeping the sound consistent without any changes in intensity. When you can do that, you know that you're using the correct amount of air.

Rolling the tongue requires more air pressure that flapping the lips, so don't expect to maintain the sound as long as you would in the lip-flapping version. This is because the tongue is flexed during the pronunciation of 'Rrrrrr'. In fact, the tongue is flexed during all consonants. It requires more air to move a flexed tongue than a relaxed pair of lips. If you keep losing the 'Rrrrrr', you're probably using too much force. Just back off on the air pressure a bit.

When creating the 'Rrrrrr' sound, see how little air pressure you need to keep the sound going. Use only the bare minimum necessary to produce the 'Rrrrrr'. If you feel the muscles under your jaw getting tight, you're probably using more air pressure than you need.

humming

The key to humming as a warm-up is to keep the sound buzzing in your hard palate and mask. If you allow the hum to fall back into your throat, you end up tiring out your voice and undermining your breath support.

When humming or singing scales, it's important to keep the back of your mouth open. Imagine a small ball sitting on the back of your tongue, or imitate the beginning of a yawn. This will help you to keep your pharynx enlarged, which enhances your tone.

Hum scales throughout your range. After five to ten minutes, start doing scales in which you hum only the first few notes of the scale and then, in mid-note, open your mouth and sing various vowels. For example: 'Hmmmmmm-awwwwww'. Then do a scale: 'Hmmmmmm-oooooo', and so on. By starting with a hum that buzzes in your hard palate and mask, you'll carry the proper resonation into the open note.

Almost any kind of scale is useful for warming up with. You don't need a piano by your side; just sing some five-note or nine-note scales throughout your range.

chapter 5

supersonic highs

I n the 1970s and '80s, heavy rock music was dominated by high-tenor singers such as Ozzy Osbourne, Robert Plant, Ian Gillan, Bruce Dickinson, Rob Halford, Bon Scott, Steven Tyler and Brian Johnson. Nearly all singers in big-time rock bands were tenors. Neighbourhood bands were placing ads looking for singers who could hit the high notes like these vocalists. But, starting in the '90s, baritones began to dominate the popular rock music scene. Nowadays, bands are usually looking for singers with more bottom end akin to Scott Stapp (Creed) and Aaron Lewis (Staind). There are very few high-note singers in popular heavy rock music, not because there aren't any out there, but because that is the current trend in the music business.

Nevertheless, when we talk about high notes, almost everybody has notes at the top of their range that they want to improve upon. Therefore, if you are a baritone reading this chapter and you think this is only for 'screamers', you are wrong – this chapter applies to anyone who wants to add another note or five to their range.

Unfortunately, there will be some notes that you will never hit because your particular voice isn't made that way. We all have a God-given voice type and overall range. Singers sometimes say they have a large range when in fact they are including all the thin, frail notes at the extremes of their range. What really matters is how high and low you can sing and sound consistently good – that defines your *working range*. This is the area you're confident will not fail you. Have you ever been singing the verse of a song, thinking ahead to a high note you're going to have to hit later in the song? It happens to everyone. But if you're nervous about that note, it probably means it isn't in your working range yet. If you're surprised when you nail a solid high note, that note isn't in your working range, either. The notes in your working range are notes you know you can hit solidly every time.

You can increase your working range. Listen to early Queensrÿche and Judas Priest albums. You'll find that both Geoff Tate and Rob Halford were singing high notes right out of the gate (using their God-given range). But the quality of their sound improved tremendously over the years, as proven by their later albums. And so it will be with you. If you're just starting to sing, your high notes will probably sound frail, but with practice they will grow fuller and more reliable, enabling you to get the most out of your range.

falsetto versus head voice

Singers often ask, 'How do I tell the difference between falsetto and head voice? I want head voice, but I'm not sure if I'm using falsetto.' As stated earlier, falsetto is a condition in which the vocal cords are left slightly open so that only the edges of them vibrate. Most of the air goes unimpeded through the opening between the cords. When only the edges resist the air, you get a light, breathy sound called falsetto. On the other hand, when the whole thickness of the cords vibrates, the voice sounds full. This is head voice. Head voice is a supported tone, needing a fair amount of air pressure. It requires more effort than falsetto. You'll feel it in the abdomen, whereas falsetto feels like a relief of pressure. In heavy rock, head voice is usually preferred because it conveys more power. It resonates primarily in the head and cuts through the music.

The difference between falsetto and head voice has nothing to do with volume – you can have a loud falsetto if you push enough air through the opening between the cords, but your head voice should always have the capability of being louder because it is a resonant tone. Head voice can be developed without loud volume. In fact, singing high notes just above a whisper while maintaining breath support is an excellent way to practise head voice.

From the following quotes, you'll see that singers are very aware of what they're doing when reaching for the high notes. While they may conceptualise the theory of singing differently, each is very aware of what a good high note feels like. This is a vital skill for a singer, the ability to gauge how well he or she is singing by feeling what's going on in his or her mouth, neck and torso. Once you can do that, you'll be able to check and correct yourself and you'll be on your way to becoming a master of your instrument.

hitting the right notes

BRUCE DICKINSON (IRON MAIDEN): 'It's about relaxing the throat at the crucial moment when your throat would tighten up, and you say, "I can't go any higher. I've got to go falsetto." It's almost like loosening the gag reflex. You don't clam up at the crucial moment. At that moment, you have to really consciously allow the power of your diaphragm to take the air right through into your nasal passages. It's like you can almost bypass the throat entirely. You have to completely relax it. Up to that point, you can squeeze your throat to make your voice sound gruff or snarly, but once you get into the really, really high registers, you have to actively relax your throat to let these high notes come out. There is much more tension in the abdomen because you've really got to get that column of air flying up. You've really got to get some power out of your abdomen. It's like you're trying to squeeze a plum through the back of your nose – that's what it feels like when you're doing one of these high notes. You're trying to squeeze this plum that's buried somewhere in the middle of your head. You're trying to squeeze it out through the top of your nose. At the same time, it almost feels like there's a string that goes from your sacrum right through your body and out the top of your head. It's like the sound is being pulled out of the top of your head. It involves the whole body.

Ripper Owens (Judas Priest): 'I'll tell you when I know I have my high notes: I'm a very loud singer, but when I can hold back physically, when I can sing softer and still have the note sound good, that's when I know that my voice is there. I don't have to push it or strain it and I can hold notes longer. A sensation I get on a lot of the long notes is that I almost black out. I think it's from a lack of oxygen. You get really dizzy and almost fall over. Sometimes it takes a couple seconds to get your bearings.'

Geoff Tate (Queensrÿche): 'I simply just visualise it, but not in a step-by-step process at all, I don't think. I'm simply involved in the song and moved by the emotions of the lyric and the music. If the music is really emotional to me it comes out in a way that is kind of... I like to think of it as not really my design. It's something that just comes out of me on some deep level that I can't really intellectualise on... I think that happens through being involved with what's going on, not so much thinking of it as "Okay, here's the chorus. Gotta get ready for it: tighten up, push, swallow afterwards..." I don't follow any procedure like that. Visualisation to me means focusing on what the song is about and what the point is that I'm trying to get across - losing oneself in it, really.'

Joe Lynn Turner (Rainbow, Deep Purple): 'What you do is you hear the note before you sing it and, all at the same time, you push down with the bottom half of your body – and that means you push down your guts. It's like going to the bathroom. You push down that way, and you pull up the other way – like a rubber band – to hit the high note. You pull the high note up while you're pushing down.'

JAMES LABRIE (DREAM THEATER): 'Your tongue should be as flat as it can and you're probably going to open your mouth more on the high notes. That's why you see a lot of singers who are below the mic, looking up to the ceiling. It's almost a natural instinct to think, "I'm gonna push it up there, so I'm gonna look up there." When I was 20 years old, I started to study opera with a lady by the name of Rosemary Patricia Burns out of Toronto. She taught people such as Yul Brynner, Tony Bennett, Bryan Adams, Corey Hart and several other singers... I remember doing exercises she would call 'The Alligator'. You know how your chin drops when you talk? Or, if you were to yell, I guarantee you that your chin would drop. Well, her method was that your chin stays still. It stays flat and you lift your head, almost like an alligator: the top of their mouth opens; the bottom stays, correct? The advantage of that is that it almost automatically pushes your notes to the top.'

RIK EMMETT (TRIUMPH): 'Head tones are often created by a tighter throat. I try to get my big mouth wide open and get the notes to drive from the top-back of my throat. High-end range was always natural and easy, but not as smooth and powerful as the bottom end.'

BRUCE HALL (ORDER OF THE ILLUMINATI/AGENT STEEL): 'You're not going to gain an octave in a day. You might gain an octave in three years. You might gain one new note every couple of months. It's a slow process, so you can't do it to the point of pain. When you start feeling pain, it's an indication that something is wrong. And you'd better stop, because your voice might break. That's my number-one recommendation. I consciously try to remember that even the very high notes are just notes. They're kind of all the same. You can't let high notes psych you out. If you know that something difficult is coming up, you can't adjust yourself for it. You have to stay doing what you're doing and arrive at that point in the same way that you would arrive anywhere else. You can't gear up for things. Here's a neat trick that Harry [Conklin of Jag Panzer] told me about: divert your energy away from your throat. You can hold your mic tighter, kick your foot into the ground or anything, and then your throat is free to react naturally.'

HARRY CONKLIN (JAG PANZER): 'High notes should be light and relaxed compared to the growly, compressed lower notes. The feeling in my head is one of controlled breathing. Hold your breath for 30 seconds, then hold for another 30 seconds, letting out tiny breaths every four to five seconds. Then hold your breath for 40 seconds, letting out short breaths here and there. This is what one feels when singing in the high register. There is a slight light-headedness and, depending on the length of the note, a little dizziness. This is normal and subsides with more practice and awareness.'

Joacim Cans (Hammerfall): 'An open throat and feeling the "cold spot" in the back of your mouth cavity, behind the hard palate, makes it easier to get the high notes. Also, singing on the tail end of the breath works for me. One important thing is that, the higher you go, the lesser the airflow, compared to the deep chest voice where the airflow is much more intense. I guess I had to work really hard to get my head voice going. My mid-range has always been strong and I try to do most of my singing in that range. When I started out as a singer, my falsetto was not there at all. That made my skills as a vocalist very limited. The best thing to do while developing your high range, as well as the real deep voice, is to isolate the falsetto. That's what I did and it really helped me gain a lot of range. It's pretty simple to do. You just have to find your "child" voice and do exercises using that voice.'

Matt Barlow (Iced Earth): 'People should realise that whenever you're working the highs, chances are you're also increasing your lows as well. You should work on both of them equally, and they'll both support each other. It's really important to increase your range in both directions because it really intensifies the power of your voice. If you can try to go as low as you can possibly go, it's helping your highs. The thing is, whenever I'm doing high notes I'm usually throwing some rasp and vibrato on it. If it was just a plain, high falsetto note it would probably be thin as shit – and sound like shit. It's really a matter of stylising. I've become a lot more comfortable on the last couple of records than I was on the first one because I've gained more knowledge about what my voice can do. But I would definitely say that if you can put some rasp and vibrato on it, especially if you're a bass-baritone vocalist, then all the better.

'It's important to sing to your strengths. Not everyone is able to sing above a high C in full voice. If you're a baritone, you probably have a different skill set from a tenor. You probably have a richer tone and more versatility in your low and mid notes. You should write songs in keys that enable your vocal attributes to shine. Singers with very high notes (high E and above) usually discover that they have these notes naturally. Then they may or may not work to make these notes fuller and more reliable. If you have a strong bottom end, you should work to optimise that. Build on your strengths.'

Ripper Owens (Judas Priest): 'I'm a firm believer that [a good range is] a thing you're born with. I mean, you can work on it, but it's a natural thing. If somebody doesn't have high notes, and they want to get them, it might be quite hard to just get high notes. It's like me learning Spanish all of a sudden: it's hard. And you know what? Why sing high notes if you don't have them? You can probably put a few in there, but just work on your chest voice and your regular voice. Why try to sing something you don't have? When I sing high notes, that's me. That's what I have.'

CHUCK BILLY (TESTAMENT): 'After singing a lot of the harder, heavy stuff, that falsetto range got lost. I still do screams, but those are more like a couple of words at a time. I don't do full songs in falsetto any more. That never really fit my style, anyway. I was always more of a power singer.'

JAMES LABRIE (DREAM THEATER): 'I believe to a certain degree that vocalists are either endowed with a very ballsy voice or they're not. You either have a very powerful voice and a really good range, or you don't. I mean, you can work on the power and range to a certain degree, but you cannot take a baritone and make him a first tenor. That doesn't mean they can't sing tenor, but if they do they'll burn out, because it's unnatural for them. So the voice has to have that natural ability to sing high.'

When going up the range, some singers have a tendency to get louder. This volume enables them to power through the break between chest and head voice. However, you should always practise your high notes at various volumes. If you have to sing highs loudly, your chest notes might become difficult to sing softly. When you limit yourself to belting, you end up losing dynamics and making your voice less interesting to listeners. You should be able to start high notes at a volume just above a whisper and still maintain a nice full sound. To help you on your way to a consistent, broad register, here are some technique-building exercises.

half-note scales

Starting at your normal speaking pitch, perform ascending half-note scales going all the way to the top. Half-notes, or semitones, are one piano key apart (counting the black keys, too). Get the first notes as full in your mouth as possible, to the point where you feel that you could almost bite into them. Then attempt to carry that sensation of fullness into the head voice. By keeping the notes close together it's easier to carry the thickness of these chest notes up to the head notes.

When you get toward the top, just touch on the very top notes. You don't need to sustain them. This is because, when you hit a note in the upper register, you are really building the whole register – the notes on the way to the top are helping to strengthen the top. For example, hitting a full, high B can actually make your high C stronger by adding the weight necessary to hit a high C. Think about it: how can you carry a thin B note into a thick C note? You can't.

ascending siren

Do the same exercise again, except this time hum the note like a siren: one continuous note, up and down. Try to keep the voice from breaking as you go into head voice. Once you're comfortable with the humming version, sing the siren on 'Ah'.

messa di voce

This is a great exercise for adding fullness to high notes. In your head voice, start at a low volume, just above a whisper. Fill your mouth with as much tone as possible. Increase the volume but not the pitch. Try to maintain the same fullness of tone you started with. Increase the volume up to about 80 per cent of your maximum volume. Don't go as loud as you can and try not to allow any cracks in your voice. Then, bring the volume down to the level at which you started. The note should maintain the same tonal quality throughout the rising and falling process. Do this on different notes throughout your chest and head voices. You'll find that your voice will probably crack at certain pitches. This is one of those exercises that very few people truly master, so don't expect to be perfect at it. It will, however, greatly improve your overall singing ability.

octave jumps

Sing a low tone in chest voice, getting your mouth as full of tone as possible, then jump up one octave into head voice, keeping the same sensation of fullness. Both your larynx and your face should remain in the same position. If you do this correctly, the high note will not feel like a stretch; it will feel just like hitting the low note, but with a little more breath pressure.

You can see that you need only a little more force on high notes than you do on low ones. That subtle difference is plenty for the small muscles of the vocal cords and larynx. You don't have to strain and push. Once you've become comfortable with taking the fullness of the low note to the head voice at various pitches, try the following: while you're hitting that high note, do scales up in your head voice, trying to keep that tone as full as possible as you move around. This will add flexibility to your high notes. If you're singing too loudly on any exercise, you'll have difficulty with flexibility. It's hard to move the voice around when you're blasting it out at full volume. The point of this version of the exercise, therefore, is to get fullness of tone at 50 to 80 per cent of your maximum volume. If you can do that, you'll have much more stamina because high-volume singing wears out the voice.

troubleshooting

If your high notes are too shrill, imagine the tone swelling in your chest and vibrating there. This will help lower the larynx without deliberate force and help add bottom to the tone.

If you're having trouble energising your high notes, you might be keeping them too low in your throat. High notes need to be lifted to the head and anchored there. To help reach those high notes, imagine aiming the voice straight up through your head. Imagine that your voice is like an arrow and your diaphragm is a bow. The bow pulls down and shoots that high note straight through the top of your head. This will give you the added lift you need to nail those notes.

If you keep cracking into falsetto through the register break, look for the following sensation to help you determine if you're on the right track:

• The notes should feel slightly squeezed as you're going through the passaggio (the passage from chest to head voice). The notes feel like they're under tight control. They resonate a little more forward in the mouth, near the soft part of the roof of your mouth just behind your front teeth. You might even have the sensation that you are biting down on the note.

If you allow the passaggio notes to spread wide open, your larynx will rise and you'll feel a loss of control. When this happens, the notes feel like they are going splat! all over the place. To correct this problem, you must learn how the passage notes should feel. Imagine that your voice is a beam of light. As you go through the break, imagine that beam leaning forward in your mouth. As you go up into the head register, imagine the beam getting straighter and straighter as you get higher and higher. When you reach the very top notes, the imaginary beam would be shooting straight up through the top of your head.

chapter 6

gods of rasp

I n the realm of heavy rock singing, there is often the need to sing with more energy and grit than in other styles of singing. While it's certainly possible to have a successful career singing entirely clean vocals, the fact remains that many singers want to know how to add a little extra 'edge' to their voices. This could involve anything from a little bit of rasp to massive guttural growls, depending on your preference and the style of music you play. This chapter talks about adding that 'monster edge' to your voice.

Different people use different terms to describe this sound: raspy, growly, gritty, dirty, rough... The terms 'edge' and 'edgy' will be used here to encompass all these kinds of singing. I like this term because it emphasises that the clean voice should be primary and the rasp should be a distortion of the edges of the note, rather than a complete distortion of the note. If you think of growling or raspy singing as a complete distortion of the note, you'll be more inclined to overdo the growling, resulting in more potential for damage to your voice. However, if you think of raspy, growly singing as adding an edge to the note, you'll tend to start clean and add the edge as necessary to get the sound you want.

Some voices seem more suited for edgy singing than others. I believe that attaining an edgy tone is possible for anyone, but the quality and nature of that sound will differ from person to person. Phil Anselmo of Pantera growls heavily, David Coverdale has a more subtle, raspy tone. Brian Johnson and Axl Rose have their own kind of raspy tones. And you, too, have a unique sound that you can develop.

how is it done?

Adding edge is all about control - you must be able to push only as much as needed to get the sound you want. If you overdo it, you'll probably wear down your voice. Edgy singing must be done with caution: if it hurts, stop! Pain does not equal gain when singing. Learn to sing the note cleanly first so that it will be strong enough to endure the punishment of adding rasp.

It's a myth that you need to tighten your throat to growl. Some singers have even said that they feel more tightness in the throat on clean notes. That's how relaxed your throat should be to get an edgy sound. Tightening will only make singing more difficult. The added power needed to get good metal edge comes from the support muscles in the abdomen, between the ribs and in the back. It has nothing to do with a clenched throat.

There are no exercises that I know of designed specifically to add edge to the voice. The best way to do it is to practise singing that way and experiment with different sounds. It might be a little uncomfortable but it should never be painful.

Remember that rasp and growl are flourishes and should be performed within the context of singing. The note comes first and the edge goes on the top. If you sing thrash metal consisting of nothing but growling, you are walking a thin line. Although there are many singers who've managed to sing like this for years, there are others you've never heard of who blew out their voice and are now out of the music business. Remember your voice type and texture and don't force it. If growling is difficult for you, try incorporating it as an embellishment rather than as your primary sound. There's nothing wrong with sounding clean. In fact, you'll notice that many great singers sing primarily cleanly and add a slight edge only for emphasis.

the pros speak

David Draiman of Disturbed has a massive growling tone. How does he do it? Does he just tighten up and push with all he's got? It's all attitude and willpower, right? Wrong. David knows what not to do. He's very aware of what it takes to growl without losing his voice. He keeps his throat open and uses the muscles in his lower back to increase his power.

DAVID DRAIMAN: 'It's hard to describe. The biggest issue is making sure that your throat is not being utilised completely. You're gonna need to use it in some way to generate that type of sound, but you should remember that it's always going to have to remain open. People try to attain a gravelly voice by closing up the throat and trying to force air through it – you're going to end up hurting yourself very, very badly. There are plenty of singers who do that and, over the course of time, develop nodes and callouses and things that affect their voice for the rest of their life.'

Rik Emmett (formerly of Triumph) is known for his soaring, clean, high voice, so what he says about raspy singing is no surprise: 'I'm not keen on it and I'm not much good at it. It makes me sound like a Rod Stewart impersonator. It doesn't suit me. The older I get, the more I value clean notes. I've always been more of a clean singer, anyway. Rasp always sounded too affected to me – pretentious somehow, like I was trying too hard. It works for others, but it's not my cup of tea.'

What about the throaty growls of Chuck Billy of Testament, one of the most successful trash metal bands of all time?

CHUCK BILLY: 'When I first started doing it, it was hurting my voice. I really noticed that, if I didn't do my vocal warm-ups and wasn't really ready to sing, I'd be hoarse the next day. I noticed I had to go through a routine to do it. Now, every time I sing I have to go through this hour-long warm-up. A lot of the technique between the two styles is different. When I sing normally, I kind of pinch the vocals and close my throat down a little bit. When I sing the death stuff, I just open it up and push a lot of diaphragm.'

GREGG ANALLA (TRIBE OF GYPSIES): 'A lot of singers have a tendency to push with the stomach – and push even harder with the throat. You're gonna do damage that way. I would say support with your abdomen and get that raspiness you want – you'll feel it in your throat – but back off of it a little bit. You'll find that the mic picks up a lot of that stuff, so you don't really have to go overboard.'

BRUCE DICKINSON (IRON MAIDEN): 'Singing fairly clean is a result of trying to keep the throat open. I can put raspiness in it just by relaxing the muscles that are keeping the throat open. It's a bit like a guitarist who has a wah-wah pedal. You only have to touch the pedal a tiny, tiny bit to produce the effect. In singing, that's the way you limit the damage.'

SEAN PECK (CAGE): 'When I'm doing the higher clean notes, I feel more contraction. I try and relax more when I'm doing the growls.'

JORNE LANDE (ARK, MILLENIUM, YNGWIE MALMSTEEN): 'That grit is something that you've got to do for a long time to make it actual. I didn't have that grit in the same sense when I was younger. When I wanted some of that grit, I had to force it, just to get a little bit of it, and used my throat in a certain way to get it in the beginning. It wasn't comfortable. But then, suddenly, I learned how to use different techniques, so I didn't think about it any more. And now it's harder to sing without grit. Now it's just there.'

GROG PREBBLE (DIE SO FLUID): 'It takes more energy to give it a lot of volume. I don't divide songs up into raspy/non-raspy sections; I use a variety of sounds between the two to do what the song requires. I think the more experienced you are, the more control you get over your voice and the more you can express with it.'

RALF SCHEEPERS (PRIMAL FEAR): 'When I sing dirty, I push more from the diaphragm, in the mid range. In the high range I work with the airflow. When I sing clean, there is more air flowing through the vocal cords but it is important to keep the diaphragm in tension. When I want to growl, I push more, even in those high ranges. That didn't come in days or months; it took years to find out how to sound crispy and how to sound clean.'

JOACIM CANS (HAMMERFALL): 'The only place I try to add some edge is in my lower range. The technique is the same, but the expressions are different. I guess the face changes when you add the edge and all the facial muscles get tense. When you find the right sensation, you'll find it doesn't take much effort to get a great voice with a nice edge to it. Never push too hard! The most important thing is to try to remain relaxed in the throat and body because if you get tense in your throat you can ruin your voice.'

You might think that heavy rock singers would throw caution to the wind and growl without discretion, but true pros are very cautious when it comes to growling. They consciously look for ways to sing with as little discomfort as possible. Certainly, raspy singing is harder on the voice than clean singing, but it can usually be done to some degree. Some singers have lyrical voices and cannot sing with rasp. Some get good rasp only on low notes, while others can add it only to high notes. Kip Winger said that he sang Winger songs in the high part of his range because that's where his voice got raspy. Learn to know where in your range you can add rasp and where you can't.

Since vocal damage is a real risk when singing rock, this is a good place to talk about common voice injuries. Following, then, are descriptions of the most common types of vocal injuries.

laryngitis

The first sign of injury is often laryngitis, which ranges from slight hoarseness to a complete loss of your voice. You might also notice pain or a lack of voice control. Laryngitis is inflammation of the larynx (voicebox). When the vocal cords are over-used, they become inflamed to protect them from further damage. It usually isn't painful, but it can be.

Laryngitis has numerous causes: excessive or improper growling, allergies, respiratory infections, singing too loudly, smoking, yelling at sporting events, working in a dusty environment, inhaling chemicals. Acute (short-term) laryngitis is what you have when you feel hoarse for a day or two after singing and can last for up to three weeks. Often it's a sign that you've misused your voice, but it can also accompany a respiratory infection. You should seek medical advice if you experience hoarseness lasting for more than two weeks or if it's accompanied by pain. If you keep losing your voice, you may have recurring acute laryngitis, which could be a sign of a more serious problem such as acid reflux disorder, a disorder in which stomach acid backs up into the larynx, irritating the vocal cords.

Treatment for acute laryngitis involves vocal rest and self-care: use the voice as little as possible, drink lots of water, take nutritional supplements and avoid environments with excessive air conditioning. It's also good to avoid caffeine and alcohol, because they dehydrate the vocal cords.

polyps

Polyps are smooth, projecting growths which can appear on many parts of the body, not just on the vocal cords. They look similar to mushrooms and interfere with the ability of the cords to close properly. The main thing to remember is that it doesn't take prolonged vocal abuse to induce polyps; they can be brought on by singing hard without first warming up. The main symptom of a polyp is hoarseness or a breathy voice. At the same time, you might have the feeling that something is caught in your throat, making you want to clear your throat frequently. Polyps must usually be removed surgically.

nodules

Nodules is the official term for nodes. A node is a small swelling on the edge of both cords that results from friction, rather like a callous. The result is that when you try to sing, the cords can't touch each other because they are prevented from doing so by the nodules. It's like trying to put your hands together with a golf ball between them. The main symptom is hoarseness or huskiness in the middle register. Singing might take more effort than normal, requiring more air pressure to sustain notes. Even speaking might be a chore. Fortunately, nodules can be removed, and voice therapy is usually the treatment of choice, while severe nodules are sometimes removed surgically. Once the nodules are gone, the voice usually returns to normal. Some nodules do not significantly interfere with vocal production: small nodules are common in rock singers and can contribute to a gritty sound.

Nodules can be caused by excessive singing. If you have laryngitis and sing regardless, you are at risk of developing nodules. Other causes include singing too loudly, having an excessively hard attack or singing a lot without breath support. These bad habits must be stopped or the nodules can recur.

contact ulcers

Slapping the vocal cords together can cause contact ulcers, which are ulcers that form due to repeated trauma. The primary symptom is the sensation of something being caught in your throat, and you might experience pain when you try to speak or sing. In some cases, you won't be able to sing at all. The treatment is usually non-invasive, involving inhaled steroids, voice therapy and an anti-reflux regimen. Surgery is used as a last resort.

final tips

In rock music, the type of edgy singing you hear is usually more intense than the slight rasp used by artists such as Rod Stewart and Bryan Adams. Slight rasp is usually produced by using less air support than normal, along with a tight throat. The heavy, edgy singing found in rock music is produced by *overdriving* the note (Brian Johnson, Rob Halford, Chuck Billy). That means keeping the throat open and using strong breath support in the abdomen and lower back. It is inherently more aggressive and fits the nature of rock music in general.

When singing with edge, you should be thoroughly warmed up first. This style of singing is damaging to the voice in both the short term and long term, but that damage can be minimised if you do it with care. The key to doing it relatively safely is to not over-constrict the throat. You might experience slight tension in your throat, but it is simply an after effect. When you growl with power, your throat might react by clamping down very slightly, but it will remain primarily open.

If growling hurts, try placing the note further forward in your mouth. Growling often hurts when you allow the note to fall too far back into the throat. You want to imagine the note projecting outwards so that the sensation of the edge is primarily in your mouth, not in your throat.

When you get a good, heavy sound going, ease up to see how much force is really necessary to produce it. You'll probably find that you can produce the same sound with far less effort than you initially thought. Of course, the more you practise, the more control you'll develop. Sing along to your favourite singers and experiment with your voice. In time, you will be able to add your own monster edge with good control and minimal effort.

chapter 7

taming the beast

More than any other chapter in this book, this one perhaps provides the deepest insight into the minds of pro singers. Some fans might think that rock singing is all about attitude and that being a rock star is all fun and games, but he singers here show that there's more to it than that. The singer in a professional band must take care of his or her voice. There are lots of ways to do this and lots of habits that pros swear by.

'There's no substitute for rest and hydration'

– Rik Emmett

This chapter consists of quotes from the pros about how to keep your voice in shape, particularly when on the road. The two most common voice-care suggestions were rest and hydration. Rest involves not talking or singing and getting plenty of sleep, while hydration involves drinking lots of water and avoiding dry environments such as rooms with air conditioning or electric heaters. It also includes the use of humidifiers and hot steam showers. Other suggestions include physical exercise and supplementation such as vitamins, teas, herbs and so on.

the pros speak
hydration

GEOFF TATE (QUEENSRŸCHE): 'Your body is your instrument, so I try to keep my body strong. I try to stay healthy. Get lots of sleep, that kind of thing. The air conditioning thing is really a problem. It's not so bad at the beginning of the tour, but once you get a few months into the tour and you get tired because you've just been singing and singing and singing, then your throat gets a little sensitive. I'm really unpopular with the band or anyone I'm travelling with because I always keep the air conditioner off. Everybody's miserable! So I tend to travel by myself nowadays. The humidifier helps. A great substitute for a humidifier is a shower in your hotel room running full blast with hot steam coming out everywhere. The whole idea is to keep your body lubricated. You don't need the humidifier so much if you drink tons and tons of water all the time, which I tend to do nowadays, because I find that it works better for me [than the humidifier]. If I haven't been taking care of myself, or it's at the end of the tour, or I've been sick, I have to do these things constantly to keep myself up so I don't miss any shows. You definitely don't want to get sick. So the best thing I've found is to drink about six or seven of those big 1.5 litre bottles of water. I always carry one around with me and that way I stay healthy and my voice stays really lubricated.'

David Draiman (Disturbed): 'Speaking in general is a lot more difficult on the voice than singing. Occasionally I'll use a humidifier. The problem is that too much humidity is no good, either. In the beginning, I used to bring the humidifier into the room and just flood the room with humidity. Then you have a good chance of aspirating a little bit of the moisture in the air; and then you end up with an irritation, which can lead to an infection in the lungs. The humidifier needs to be cleaned constantly because it can spew forth airborne bacteria. It's not a simple thing. It is always important to keep yourself hydrated and humidity in the environment will certainly help you to do that, but it is not a be-all and end-all by any means.'

Joe Lynn Turner (Rainbow, Deep Purple, Yngwie Malmsteen): 'You've gotta keep the voice moist. Now, I bought this little humidifier no bigger than a cell phone. It has a cup that goes around your nose and your mouth. I just breathe it in and out, to wet the voice and loosen the sinuses. Usually I'll do that before a show, for a good 30 minutes. Sometimes, during a drum solo or something, I'll run backstage and take a couple of shots of that. And you've gotta drink a lot of water. I've done enough drugs and drink to know that both of those will drain the life out of your organs. Alcohol is a drying agent. Just put rubbing alcohol on your skin and see what it does. Now, if you drink it, what the hell do you think it's doing to your insides?'

Rob Rock (Warrior): 'I try to sleep with a humidifier in the room and on the bus because it keeps my voice moist and lets it heal. I don't drink and smoke, either. I try to eat well, but not just before the show. Keeping the voice in the best shape is the top priority for me on the road because the fans deserve the best you can give.'

Matt Barlow (Iced Earth): 'I would definitely say don't stay up and party all night. You're a vocalist. You carry your instrument around with you. A guitar player doesn't carry his instrument into a smoky bar and pour alcohol all over it, and neither should you. Believe me, man, I smoked for many years and I loved smoking. I absolutely loved it. I also like to drink beer. But on tour, you can't do it. Wait until your day off, then indulge.'

JOE COMEAU (ANNIHILATOR): 'I bring a kettle with me. I get some hot water going a half-hour before the show. I don't drink coffee or tea. I just drink hot water. Then I'll keep that pot up on-stage. I try to get a road crew guy to watch it for me, because it's important. It really helps loosen things up.'

JOACIM CANS (HAMMERFALL): 'Drink a lot of water before, during and after the show. Keep in mind that you shouldn't drink cold water – it should be room temperature at all times. As a vocalist, you have to be the boring one and go to bed without partying every night. Alcohol really damages your voice and you should also stay away from too many cups of coffee.'

KIP WINGER: 'The big myth in singing is this hot-tea-and-honey bullshit. That's the biggest myth there ever was. The best thing you can do for your voice, in any circumstance, is to drink cold water. I drink iced water.'

rest

RAY ALDER (FATES WARNING): 'Sleep is the key. On tour I probably get at least ten hours a day, at the absolute least. I mean, after a show you don't get to bed until four or five in the morning, normally. After that, you just try to sleep as much as you can. Soundcheck isn't until about five or six o'clock, so I normally get up around two or three and get something to eat.'

JOE LYNN TURNER (RAINBOW, DEEP PURPLE): 'The main thing is that you try to get sleep. That's the most difficult thing on the road. For a singer, it's like if you had a pea under your mattress last night, you felt it.'

JAMES LABRIE (DREAM THEATER): 'One of the most important things for a vocalist is tons of sleep. Every vocalist who's out there touring should try to get at least ten hours of sleep a night.'

BRUCE DICKINSON (IRON MAIDEN): 'Don't be a hero. Get a good doctor, one who's not scared of your manager. One that will say, "You must not sing for at least ten days," or however long it is. And don't say, "Oh, ten days, that means seven days." Ten days means ten days. Take the doc's advice.'

supplementation

CHUCK BILLY (TESTAMENT): 'All those little tiny things you never think you'd do, you end up doing because over the years you realise they help. Before, I would just drink through the show, drink after, drink before. But I take more care of myself now. I drink a metric shake when I come off-stage. I take vitamins before I go on-stage to keep me going.'

James LaBrie (Dream Theater): 'Take vitamins like B12 and zinc. I take zinc once a day because it's incredibly good for the voice. It rebuilds the tissues quickly. The B12 gives you energy. On top of that, I'm drinking juice and tons of water all the time.'

Ripper Owens (Judas Priest): 'I take licorice root with me. Black licorice is good for your throat. Everybody would know that because it's in cough drops. And Throat Coat Tea is filled with licorice. I used to use this throat spray that was good for you. I couldn't find it any more so I decided to make my own. I dropped about four or five drops of licorice root into a little spray bottle and put just a drop of lemon in. So I just sprayed this stuff in my throat. I actually had it on-stage with me this tour.'

physical fitness

Ripper Owens (Judas Priest): 'I try to swim. I like to hit the steam room. I like to run on the treadmill. Swimming really seems to help me a lot. It's great exercise.'

Andy Franck (Brainstorm, Symphorce): 'I believe that your vocal fitness depends on your physical fitness. Since I do a lot of jogging and so on, I never had any problems with my voice on a tour.'

In the individual interviews in the next chapter of this book, you'll find more tips on vocal stamina, including personal stories from singers who have injured their voice and what was done to treat them.

chapter 8

the pros speak

Ray Alder

Ray is the vocalist for Fates Warning, one of the first and most successful progressive metal bands in the world. Ray has a unique sound with a good range and sings well both cleanly and with a rough edge.

BILL: Who influenced you as a singer?

RAY: You've probably heard this a million times: Rob Halford. As a kid I heard *Unleashed In The East*, and it changed my life. I was only 14 years old, but still it was amazing. I'd have to say Steve Perry as well. Those are my biggest influences.

BILL: When did you start singing?

RAY: I was 15 years old. My brother started a band in Dallas, Texas. Somehow I got a hold of some wine and started singing. I think the very first song we did was 'Whiskey Man' by Molly Hatchet. After that, my brother moved to San Antonio, so I ended up joining the band.

BILL: When you're on the road, is there anything specific you do to keep your voice from wearing out?

RAY: I think one of the main things for me is to not talk so much after the show. I know the way I sing, my style, is not correct. I actually took lessons in '91 from the same woman who taught James Labrie from Dream Theater.

BILL: Mary Elizabeth Burns?

RAY: Yeah. So I took lessons from her for like maybe two weeks, mainly because of the fact that I was throwing my voice out all the time. On tour, you play eight or nine shows in a row with a day off. Then you play eight or nine more shows in a row. Obviously it takes its toll. It's a sad thing, but it's always on the singer. Everybody else can do whatever they want. But for me the worst thing is to talk a whole lot after the show. Alcohol is an absolute killer. Never drink before you go on-stage because it kills everything. I recently quit smoking. I smoked for 16 years and I just quit for the last six months. The patch works.

BILL: Have you noticed any difference?

RAY: No! [Laughs] No difference whatsoever! I feel a little better, though. Anyway, alcohol and talking after the show are the worst things. Other than that, I just do what I do. As a kid, I really abused my voice. As I'm getting older, I don't have the stamina that I used to. My voice used to recover after about a day. Now it's not as fast. I really have to take care of myself on the road. You know, touring in the winter is bad because there's nothing but dry, hot air on the bus. There's nowhere to get away from it. Even if you put a humidifier in the back of the bus, the moisture's still gonna get sucked down through the door, so you're screwed. Yeah, dry heat kills your voice. The main thing is to keep the bus cool and not have the heat on as much.

BILL: How important is sleep?

RAY: Abso-LUTE-ly important! Sleep is the absolute key. On tour I probably get at least ten hours a day. I mean, after a show you don't get to bed until four or five in the morning. After that you just try to sleep as much as you can. Soundcheck isn't until about five or six o'clock. So I normally get up around two or three and get something to eat. Then, I'm probably the opposite of most singers because I try to talk and sing a bit about an hour after I wake up, just to get my voice back in shape before soundcheck.

BILL: Have you ever damaged your voice in any way?

RAY: Yeah, actually I have. When I was 16 we were doing some bar sets. We did about three sets that night and I lost my voice for like a week. After that I thought, 'I'd better take it easy and not sing so much any more.' I did have some problems for a while. I was seeing a voice doctor, the same doctor as John Bush.

BILL: Dr Sugarman?

RAY: Yeah, Joseph Sugarman. I was having some problems with my voice at one point. I didn't know what the hell was going on. No matter what I would do, my high notes were gone. I really, really had to work to get to my high notes. Actually, my very high notes were fine. It was my mid-highs. It was a fucking nightmare. So I busted out the wallet and went to see Sugarman. He's a great guy. I'd recommend him to any singer. You should see all the platinum and gold records on his wall. I mean, everybody goes to see him. He's the man. So I was really scared, and I went to him, and I was diagnosed with acid-reflux disease. Even when I didn't know it, I had heartburn, and it was constantly irritating my vocal cords, which was dumping my voice down to a lower register. So he put me on these really hardcore antacids that I have to take at night before I go to bed. And things are so much better. But now I really have to watch what I eat. I can't drink orange juice any more. I can't eat spicy foods. And I obviously had to quit smoking because it was compounding everything.

BILL: What about your range? Has it always been what it is now, or has it improved over the years?

RAY: I wouldn't say it's improved. I'm 33 years old now. On the first record I did with Fates, I was 18 years old, so obviously my voice was a lot higher then. It was a lot easier. But after a while it felt kind of silly singing that high, you know? It was cool back in '88 because everybody was doing it. And I was a huge fan of John Arch, the old Fates Warning singer. So I wanted to be like John Arch, but I started coming into my own and started realising that there's more to singing than just singing high. There's melody and emotion, and so much more. So I changed my voice a little bit. As I got older, I kind of found my niche.

BILL: Technique-wise, how is singing clean high notes different from singing them with a growl?

RAY: It's a lot different. Heavy singing is more taxing on the vocal cords because you're tensing up the throat and you're pushing a lot harder. But some people just sing that way. It's normal for them. But for me to do that, I have to try. So, for me, I would lose my voice if I did that every single night. But I'm sure I'd get used to it if I had to do it.

BILL: So, for you, it involves more pushing from below?

RAY: Well, since I'm not the most correct singer in the world, I tend to use my throat a lot more than I should. So when I do the growly thing, that's exactly where it goes. That's probably why I can't do it for too long. But when I sing live, I always tend to sing a little bit heavier than I would on the record. Normally I have a pretty clean voice, but on tour you have a lot more raw emotion coming out and things happen. I like that. That's kind of why I wanted to do a solo record. I wanted to do something with that style of vocals and it came out great. It was an outlet to sing completely different and not have to worry about being so clean all the time.

BILL: How about high notes? Is there a change in technique when you go into the upper part of your range?

RAY: Yeah. I was discussing this with another voice coach before. You have a chest voice, a head voice and a nasally voice. My high notes are more of a head voice. It sort of resonates. It's really strange. I can't really explain it.

BILL: Where do you feel the sensations?

RAY: I feel it behind my eyes. When I was taking lessons with Mary Burns, she was saying, 'Do you feel this here? Where's this note? Where's that note?' Finally, I realised that my high notes are behind my eyes. It's the weirdest thing.

BILL: Does the sensation vary? Usually, the higher you go, the higher the sensations go.

RAY: Yeah, it actually does. It moves up and out, to the top of the head. But I usually don't sing that high any more, so the sensation is lost.

BILL: Do you tend to be a loud singer?

RAY: Very loud. I'm very much compressed on record, and live as well, because I can go from one level to the next right away. I've always tended to be a really, really loud singer, which is probably one reason I was throwing my voice out when I was so young.

BILL: What do you do to warm up before a show?

RAY: I try to find a quiet spot. The best place for me is a bathroom or a room without carpets that has some sort of natural reverb. That's the best because you can hear it in your head. It just feels better; you don't have to push as hard. I think that, when I'm in a dry room, I tend to push a lot harder to hit the notes. I go from the lows to the highs, move around a little bit, just try to warm the voice up, do a couple of scales of my own discovery. I just pretty much make them up. Again, I probably do the wrong thing, but I always drink warm liquids, like coffee with a lot of sugar in it. For me, it feels good to go on-stage with tons of energy.

BILL: Do you warm up with any songs from the set?

RAY: I might do a couple of lines in the songs, ones that are particularly hard or something, but my warm-up really only consists of four or five minutes. It's not much.

BILL: How soon before the show?

RAY: Maybe about 10 or 15 minutes before the show.

BILL: And that works? You're ready to go?

RAY: I don't know if it works, but that's what I do.

BILL: But have you ever had any trouble with your voice?

RAY: Oh yeah, obviously I have. Being on tour, you kind of lose your voice. There are points when you know you aren't going to hit a certain note, so you just work on that. I'll be like, 'Okay, well I can't hit that note. I can't hit the transition because my voice is so fried at this point. And I don't want to burn it out because I have six more shows in front of me.' So you find another way around it. You'll change a couple of notes or something like that. Sometimes you just have to.

BILL: Okay, so you change the melody. Do you ever just let the crowd sing the chorus?

RAY: [sighs] I guess you've heard that one already, huh? Yeah, abso-fucking-lutely, man. But the crowd likes that. It could make for a great show. It could also make for a disaster if they don't know who the hell you are and you're up there pointing your microphone at them. If you lose your voice while you're on the road, you're in hell. Normally, I can call my doctor. I can say [in a soft, breathy voice], 'Um...I need your help.' And he's like, 'Oh my God, what did you do?' Normally they can get you a prescription for something. Cortisone is like God to a singer. I'm like, 'Okay, I'm gonna call this place and go down and get a cortisone shot,' and it shrinks your vocal cords up in an hour.

The whole time I've been in the band, I think I had to cancel only three shows because I absolutely lost my voice. I would get a cold. I think I always get a cold on the road, at least once. It lasts about two days, so I have about two shows that really suck. Then it just builds back up. That whole term 'the show must go on' is absolutely true. The weird thing is, if you're a guitar player, bass player or drummer and you kind of fuck up, no one really notices. But if you're a singer in a rock band and you don't sound as good as you normally do, you think you're the worst-sounding fucking guy in the world: 'Everyone thinks I suck! Ahhh, this is gonna suck!' But then, at the end of the night, people come up to you and say, 'You rock, man! You're the best singer in the world!' When you hear these things, you think, 'Couldn't you tell?' Even guys in the band are like, 'I really couldn't tell.' But you in your own mind think you had a shitty show. But only maybe five per cent of the audience really notices.

BILL: Is some of that self-doubt related to the way the notes feel when you're sick? I mean, it feels different from what you're used to, even though it sounds pretty close to normal?

RAY: Yeah. And when you're improvising things on the fly, your confidence is gone sometimes because you're not doing things the way you'd normally do it. Normally you're just like a machine – you just get on and pound it out - but if you have to start thinking about how you're singing, sometimes you'll forget lyrics, or you'll forget where the hell you're gonna go next in the middle of improvising a line or something. All of a sudden you're two keys down from where the hell you're supposed to be. After the fact, you're left wondering, 'Damn, I should have done that a bit better.' You're thinking, 'Oh, I should I have done this note. What am I going to do with the next note?' And you're thinking all of this *while you're still singing the damn song!*

There's no bigger blow to your confidence than having to think about where the hell you're gonna go while you're singing. I'll tell you, I've actually forgotten lyrics because I started thinking about what the hell I was doing. It's only happened a couple of times, though. Normally you're just in a groove. It all comes pretty naturally, like walking. But as soon as you start thinking, 'Left step, right foot, left foot...'

BILL: Next thing you know, you're breaking stride.

RAY: Yep.

BILL: Any final advice for aspiring singers?

RAY: Just stick with it and know where you want to go. If you think you sound silly, you probably do. You hear a lot of singers nowadays that just want to sing really high, and there's really no melody to it, no soul. In order to be a singer, you have to be able to feel what you're singing. Understand the lyrics. You really have to feel it deep within to make an impact. Feel the music – and don't try to be a rock star.

Gregg Analla

Gregg is known for his current work with Latin-rock band Tribe Of Gypsies and previous work with progressive metal band Seventh Sign. Gregg, who is full-blooded Pueblo Indian, is also an accomplished artist and sculptor. His singing voice is smooth and melodic.

BILL: Who influenced you as a singer?

GREGG: I'd have to say my favourite singer is Glenn Hughes. Influentially, I'd have to say Ian Gillan, Geoff Tate and Kate Bush. Definitely Rob Halford – and Bruce Dickinson, too. That pretty much covers it.

BILL: Have you ever taken vocal lessons?

GREGG: Actually, I had one lesson. I looked up this guy – I can't remember his name right now, but he taught the likes of Michael Jackson and Klaus Meine. I think it was 60 bucks for a half-hour. He was kind of like a militant. He was a real nice guy when I was talking to him, but as soon as the lessons started he turned into this totally different person. He was pretty much cracking the whip over me. But halfway through the lesson, he cancelled his next lesson. He said, 'I'm gonna give you an hour for free.' So we continued...and I couldn't figure out why. Then he said, 'How old are you?' I said, 'I'm 26.' He said, 'You shouldn't have this voice. The frequencies you are singing in, usually males lose these frequencies at about 20 or 21. That's why I extended your lesson. I'm trying to figure out what you've been doing.' So after I left the lesson, I figured, 'I'm not going to do any of these scales' because it would inhibit me and make me lose the voice I was still carrying at that point. I figured I must have been doing something right, so I didn't want to mess with what I was doing.

BILL: If it ain't broke, don't fix it.

GREGG: Right. That's the stance I took on it.

BILL: How important is breath support?

GREGG: Breathing is very important. The way you structure a song, sometimes you have to put in places where you have to breathe. With rock, the arrangement is pretty straightforward, but it's definitely important. I don't do any breath exercises *per se*. My voice is pretty much natural. Both my parents sang. My father was in the choir in the Air Force and my mother used to sing for a rock 'n' roll band back in the doo-wop days. So I attribute my voice to both of their talents.

BILL: How do you warm up for a show?

GREGG: I don't actually do much warming up. I like to structure the set so that some of the songs where I don't have to use a lot of aggression or strength are at the beginning of the set, so the whole set is kind of like a warm-up. At the end I can lay out some of the heavier vocal techniques. I find that, when I do warm-up, it tends to take away from the end of the show, because by then my voice is tired.

BILL: When you're on the road, what do you do to protect your voice?

GREGG: Rest is the most important thing. I'm sure a lot of singers say that. When you're tired, it definitely shows in your voice. I basically just listen to my body. If my voice is particularly dry that day, I go toward a little bit greasier food. A good greasy hamburger, I find, will coat my throat and make it easier for me to sing if I wake up with a dry throat. It's totally weird. I try to stay away from heavier foods prior to a show - foods like chicken and mashed potatoes - because they're hard to digest. When you try to breathe in, your food is like a brick in your stomach.

BILL: I assume you don't eat right before a show, either.

GREGG: No, I try to eat at least five hours before the show.

BILL: Do you smoke?

GREGG: Uh...not cigarettes [laughs]. I get high occasionally.

BILL: Do you do that before a show?

GREGG: Never before a show. Always after. If I do get high before a show, it definitely does affect the vocal performance. I stay away from that.

BILL: Besides sleep and diet, are there any other things you use to keep your voice in shape?

GREGG: Well, a lot of water is very important. My advice to singers would be to pay attention to your body. I mean, one singer I met drank nothing but Dr Pepper when he sang. He said that's what helped him through the show. I worked with a producer named Chris Mintos, who produced Sammy

Hagar, KISS, Whitesnake. His wife was a singer as well and she had all these teas out. She had lemon and honey, the typical protocol you hear singers talk about. I started singing and drinking the tea and I couldn't sing. They were freaking out on me and I was embarrassed. I was like, 'I don't know what's wrong.' I said, 'Let's go get beer.' We panicked and got all these different beers — light ones, dark ones. I drank the beer and I could sing like normal. So what I usually do when I sing live — I've found a combination that really works — I drink Heineken, and it clears the phlegm from my throat. If I find that my throat starts getting dry, I find a good liquor like Rumplemintz or ouzo. It helps in coating my throat.

BILL: People will eat that advice up. Any chance to drink more beer. It's like, 'Well, I have to drink it! It's for my voice!'

GREGG: I hate to sound like the typical rock guy – 'I gotta get drunk!' – but in my circumstance, that works. But I sip that hard stuff; I don't do shots of it.

BILL: How do you improvise on a bad-singing day? Do you *have* bad-singing days?

GREGG: Yeah, occasionally.

BILL: Have you ever damaged your voice?

GREGG: Twice. I just ended up pushing a bit too hard. Once was years ago during a live show, during the cover-band days. We were pushing it pretty hard seven nights a week for about a month. You can't do that. The best thing for that is just to not speak for at least a couple of days. The last time was last year with Tribe Of Gypsies. We were going for a heavier feel and my mistake was I drank wine. It was dry red wine and it dried out my throat. We went for some aggressive parts of these songs and I was really screaming hard, and it almost felt like my vocal cord slipped or something. I could feel it internally. It was like a pop in my vocal cords. There was a bit of pain in it and I stopped at that point. I attribute that injury to not following my protocol: not drinking enough water and drinking that wine.

GREGG: This is really important for any singer: preparation before you go on the road. Rehearsals are important. Your first day of rehearsal, you're not going to make it through a two-hour set. I don't think anybody should push themselves that hard. A two-week span of rehearsal period is great. During that time, I go in and sing until I feel my voice getting tired, then I stop. It might be only four or five songs that I can sing.

The next night, I do the same thing, and maybe I can sing seven songs. Gradually, I work my way into singing the full set. If you push yourself too hard the very first night of rehearsals, it's gonna damage the rest of your two weeks, and your rehearsal time is gonna be for naught. I call that getting into a groove, because the muscles get used to hitting all those notes. That's why warming up before a show doesn't really matter to me. Once I reach that point, I've already reached the point where my voice can just fall into that groove. I try not to deviate too much from the groove, just keep it the same every night. Not exactly the same – improvisation is great – but when I start to improvise, it's usually toward the middle of the tour because your voice is used to all the songs at that point.

BILL: That's improvisation by choice, but are there days when you find that your voice isn't quite there?

GREGG: Oh, right.

BILL: And how do you make changes to make it through that show?

GREGG: Usually just shorter notes. If the notes are really heavy notes, I'll try to sing with less intensity and move the mic closer to my mouth. Or if I find that I'm losing control toward the ends of the notes, then I pull the mic away toward the end of the notes – people don't notice it as much.

BILL: Has your range changed over the years?

GREGG: It was a little bit higher before. I noticed that, after damaging my vocal cords both times, I did lose some frequencies, but I attribute that to being a part of life. I mean, as you get older you are gonna lose some frequencies, so I don't take it to heart that much. Nobody wants to hear you screaming like a banshee at 50, anyway.

BILL: Do you have any advice for singers on how to improve their range?

GREGG: How I learned all my stuff was just basically mimicking things - not just singing the song like normal; I would actually try to imitate every aspect of how they sing a song, whether it be Bon Scott, Bruce Dickinson, Geoff Tate or Ian Gillan. I found that it made me a better singer because I could put the different aspects of each singer into my own vocal techniques. You know how some vocalists start their notes or end their notes different?

BILL: Yeah.

GREGG: Or each pronounces things differently? I would just take little bits here and there and apply them to my style. That was basically my schooling, really, researching and listening to other vocalists and trying to mimic exactly what they do.

BILL: Okay, let's talk about high notes. Do you use any physical sensations that help you know that you're in the groove?

GREGG: Oh yeah, definitely. You can feel vibrations in your skull, and usually the higher notes resonate along the forehead and in the temples.

BILL: When you go into the high range, do you tend to sing louder?

GREGG: Yes. The vocal teacher I was talking about earlier told me that that was wrong, that I should sing with less force on the higher notes and more force on the lower notes, but sometimes, in order to get those notes, you do have to push a little bit.

BILL: After all, this is rock 'n' roll, man!

GREGG: Yeah, exactly. The adrenaline's going. The intensity of the moment is there. The people are screaming along with you. I don't see anything wrong with that. I think it's fun.

BILL: A lot of singers want to achieve a raspy or gravelly sound. Do you think it depends on voice type or can anybody learn to do that?

GREGG: I think anybody can learn to do that eventually. I think it just goes with naturally falling into the groove. You can't go straight to rehearsals the first day and go 'Grrraaahhh!'. I would say to slowly work yourself up to the raspy voice over a period of time. Get used to your regular singing voice first and then start applying the raspiness in little spurts here and there when you need to. The more you do that, the more your voice is gonna be able to fall into that groove. In order to keep that raspiness, you have to be singing constantly. That's really very important. But if you overdo it, you're going to lose your voice. There's a really fine line between '[in an English accent] stupid and clever', as Spiñal Tap would say.

BILL: Definitely. For you, physically, what's the difference between singing with a rasp and singing clean? Is there anything that you do deliberately to get that sound?

GREGG: Yeah. I push more with my abdomen. Obviously there's a lot of stress on the vocal cords. A lot of singers have a tendency to push with the stomach and push even harder with the throat, but you're gonna do damage that way. I would say support with your abdomen and get that raspiness you want – you'll feel it in your throat – but back off of it a little. You'll find that the mic picks up a lot of that stuff, so you don't have to go overboard.

Matt Barlow

Matt's fierce voice has powered the monster metal band Iced Earth since 1995. Matt is a bass-baritone who is able to sing strong falsetto notes in addition to booming low notes. Iced Earth continues to be one of the most uncompromising and dynamic bands in metal.

BILL: Who influenced you, and how did you first get started as a singer?

MATT: Probably my biggest influence was my brother's music, and that would be primarily hard rock and heavy metal. He's five years my senior, so he definitely influenced me. I was listening to country music and Elvis. I was always into music and entertaining even before I really tried to start singing, back when I was a teenager, singing in choral groups in school. We started up a stage band in my school. I was one of 20 or 30 singers. They had a primary band and everybody else would take turns singing different kinds of songs. Most of the time, I ended up doing country tunes because, at that point, that's what my voice was suited for.

Actually, I'm glad I went that way first rather than trying to sing the heavier stuff I was really into, because when you're a teenager your voice is not ready for that kind of stress. You're going through puberty and your voice is changing enough, and I was untrained. I mean, I used to get sore throats and stuff, which shouldn't be happening - even if you're a professional vocalist, you shouldn't be getting a sore throat because of your singing. Then I formed a band with my brother, and we were doing mostly thrash-metal stuff. After that, I moved to Florida and got hooked up with Iced Earth.

At that point, I still hadn't had a whole lot of professional training, although my sister-in-law has a degree in voice and music and she gave me some lessons. She's trained in operatic vocals, and that's not always necessary when you're doing this kind of music. It's a cool thing to do, but opera is more geared toward stage performance without any kind of miking. It's a totally different animal. From what I have done in theatre, it's all about projection, and rock 'n' roll is more about doing different things with your voice at lower volumes. Not that operatic singing is totally without dynamics, but it's not like rock 'n' roll. Another vocal instructor that I had, named Al Cohen, actually taught me quite a few things about that, about doing things with your voice that don't require such a large volume and not having to project as much but utilising your entire instrument.

BILL: So you've had lessons from him and your sister-in-law. Anybody else?

MATT: Yeah, I've actually had lessons here in Indiana as well. I think that as many outside opinions you can get on your voice, the better. I take lessons from everybody I come in contact with, as far as professional singers and voice instructors go. If anybody can give me some information, all the better. I mean, I've taken lessons from Jon [Schaffer], who is the main songwriter in our band. When he tells me how he wants a song to sound, or he gives me an example, then I take that and try to create a unique sound. Jim Morris, our producer for the last four or five records, he's constantly giving me lessons, and that's a cool thing. Certainly, in a recording atmosphere he knows what he's doing. He's the guy who knows what people's voices can do with a microphone. Sometimes you need to look on the outside to find some different influences other than just a vocal instructor.

BILL: So when you're in the studio, do you sing differently from the way you do on-stage?

MATT: Yeah, I definitely do. On-stage, you have to use different tools because you have a set amount of time that you have to sing, and you have to perform, too. In the studio, it's mostly repetition, stopping and starting again. Stage stuff is straight through. On-stage, I tend to do a lot more support with the diaphragm and use more vibrato, which really helps, especially in a live situation. It helps you grab notes. It really helps you keep in pitch and it gives your diaphragm the workout it needs. It makes your diaphragm work for you so you don't burn out your throat. The toughest thing in the studio is all that repetition. That's what burns out my voice: stacking vocals. And sometimes you have a mind block where you can't get a part right and you have to do it over and over. When that happens, we usually just stop and do something else for a while, then come back to it.

BILL: Let's talk a little about technique. Do you tend to sing loudly?

MATT: I think it depends on where the note is. I am a bass-baritone, so usually, when I go higher up the scale, I need to go higher in volume because I'm pushing more air out. I'm really clenching and stretching the cords.

BILL: You do some fairly high stuff for a baritone.

MATT: Yeah, falsetto is a beautiful thing. You can do a lot of things while recording to really make things sound differently. It's a matter of mixing things, matching up volumes, things like that. It's not cheating because you're actually hitting the notes. But if you've got good mics and your levels are set, you can do some really killer things that normally you can't do if you're singing to yourself because you can't hear all those cool things you can do with your voice. It's a misconception that people think vocalists are using the full voice all the time.

BILL: What part of your range is the most troublesome for you?

MATT: Probably the area right between the chest and head voice. It's a tricky part. That's always something that you constantly have to work on. The more you sing, the smoother the transition is. People should realise that, whenever you're working the highs, chances are you're also increasing your lows as well. You should work on both of them equally and they'll both support each other. It's really important to increase your range in both directions, because it really intensifies the power of your voice. If you can try to go as low as you can possibly go, it's helping your highs.

BILL: How do you warm up for a performance?

MATT: I don't really warm up a lot before a performance, especially if it's within a tour, because you can really warm up too much and burn yourself out. The first couple of shows, I try to do your basic scales – do, re, mi – but a few shows into it, whenever you're playing a two-hour show, that's enough practice for one night. You can do a few scales before you go on, but don't do a half-hour's worth of warm-ups – it's really redundant. The best thing to do if you're performing a lot is to keep a lot of liquid in you. You've got to make sure that your vocal cords are moist and your entire mouth is moist. Just concentrate on that, because your body is already tuned up. I would say to definitely make sure that your ears don't get fried, because your ears are just as important in singing as your voice.

BILL: I would imagine that you don't put your most difficult song first in the set, right?

MATT: No, not normally. [The band] have some sympathy for me. We really try to work into it. It also helps the drummer.

BILL: On the road, what other things do you do to keep your voice going?

MATT: My main thing is sleep – and no talk. Don't feel like you've gotta talk to everybody. Sometimes you'll be asked to do in-stores and all that stuff, but it helps to take a couple hours out of the day to not talk. Talking is the worst thing that you can do for your singing voice.

BILL: How much sleep do you think is adequate?

MATT: The thing is, when you're touring, you can sleep all day. I would definitely say don't stay up and party all night. You're a vocalist. You carry your instrument around with you everywhere. A guitar player doesn't carry his instrument into a smoky bar and pour alcohol all over it, and neither should you. Believe me, man, I smoked for many years and I loved smoking. I absolutely *loved* it! I also like to drink beer. But on tour, you can't do it. Wait until your day off, then indulge. I get sick on every tour, and if I drank and smoked I would never recover. Because I'm not, my recovery is probably two or three days. Knock on wood, I've never missed a show because of illness.

BILL: So I guess you've never damaged your voice.

MATT: Well, I can't say that I've never damaged my voice. But you can do a lot of things when you're sick. My sister-in-law is a good example of that. She sings church gigs and stuff. I've seen her barely be able to talk, but she'll warm up and do her gig. Then, after she was done, she could still barely talk. It's totally different tools that you use for talking and for singing.

BILL: How about growling and raspy singing? Did that come naturally to you?

MATT: It's something you have to work on. It wasn't really natural for me, but the cool thing is experimentation, just playing around with your voice. I mean, now it feels totally natural for me to do it. The important thing is to know your instrument's limitations but don't limit your instrument. You can definitely overdo something and destroy yourself, but at the same time you don't want to be afraid to experiment with things.

BILL: Is there any change in technique when you sing with growl?

MATT: Yeah. This goes against all classical training, but the growl is definitely more up in the throat area. Classical training tells you to loosen everything up and belt it out, but to growl you have to do it a little bit differently. But if it hurts, you're doing something wrong and you should stop what you're doing immediately.

BILL: So even when you first started, it didn't hurt?

Matt: No, because I didn't allow it to. If it felt like it was wrong, I did something else. A sore throat doesn't do anything for you. I knew there was a safe way to do it because so many had done it before me. I can't tell anybody how to do it, because everybody's voice is different. It depends on your voice. I mean, a lot of heavy-metal singers are in a tenor range, so I'm sure I've got to do something different than what those other guys do.

Bill: Let's move on to the topic of breath support.

Matt: Diaphragm, diaphragm, diaphragm! Al Cohen taught me a lot about how important breath support is. He concentrated on how, with breath support, you can do a lot of different things. In the studio you can make lower, breathier notes sound cooler if you're supporting. I think it's the number-one thing to concentrate on. After you get that tool mastered, you can start experimenting, playing around with different mouth positions and stuff like that. Al used to tell me, 'Imagine you're holding an egg in your mouth. That's the way your mouth position should be.' But often, different stuff is cooler. Holding your jaw tight and having a lot of teeth in there, that can make for a cool sound. Whatever works in a particular situation is the best thing.

Bill: Let's talk about high notes. Hitting high notes can be difficult, especially for a baritone.

Matt: The thing is, whenever I'm doing high notes, I'm usually throwing some rasp and vibrato on it. If it was just a plain, high falsetto note, it would probably be thin as shit and sound like shit. It's really a matter of stylising. I've become a lot more comfortable on the last couple of records than I was on the first one because I've gained a lot more knowledge about what my voice can really do. But I would definitely say that, if you can put some rasp and vibrato on your voice, especially if you're a bass-baritone vocalist, then all the better.

Bill: So has your range increased over the years?

Matt: Yeah. Yeah, definitely.

Bill: Where do you tend to feel the high notes?

Matt: Right in my sinuses, behind my nose and eyes. Sometimes, when I'm doing super-duper highs, I actually get a bit of a headache. It's almost like brain freeze.

Bill: Do you use a visualisation techniques, such as imagining the note going through the top of your head or anything like that?

MATT: No. If there's a high note I need to hit, I might think about it beforehand and tell myself, 'Okay, here it comes.' Usually, I try to look ahead so I'm aware of what's coming up. That way, I can be prepared for it.

Chuck Billy

Chuck's powerful baritone voice has powered the legendary American thrash-metal band Testament since 1987. Chuck has the quintessential thrash-metal voice: strong, rough and distinctive.

BILL: So when did you start singing?

CHUCK: It was 1979 or so. My brother was in a band and they didn't have a singer. I actually was a guitar player since about sixth grade. Then, one night at rehearsal, they said, 'Here, why don't you sing the lyrics?' From that day forward, I was their singer. Then I actually took some vocal lessons out in the city, some private lessons. Then I went to college for a few years and took theory and vocals. After that, I went back out to Berkley to Judy Davis. She was a well-known singing teacher who taught people from Lucille Ball to Eddie Money to Eric Martin and Frank Sinatra. She was, like, 73 years old.

BILL: Was it helpful?

CHUCK: Oh, totally. It was a group class, though; it wasn't one-on-one. I learned from everybody else's mistakes. After I did all those lessons, I started playing around in local bands. It was the early '80s, when more melodic vocals were in. Then, around late 1984, Steve Souza, the singer for Exodus, he was in the band Legacy and grew up in the same town as I did – he was friends with my little brother, basically – and he said, 'I'm leaving Legacy to be in Exodus. They need a singer. You should check them out.' So I tried out and got the job. They already had a record contract on the table, but the company was waiting to see what the new singer sounded like, so I kind of walked right into a deal. Then we changed the name to Testament.

BILL: Who was influencing you as a singer?

CHUCK: Back then it was Ronnie James Dio, Halford, Bruce Dickinson, all the old-school singers. The melodic stuff was popular in those days, bands like Ratt and Dokken. It kind of helped me in terms of putting melody in the metal, like we do.

BILL: Do you sing loud?

CHUCK: Yeah. I've got to sing pretty hard. I didn't at first because I didn't know how to control it, but once I got my control down and confidence in my voice as I built it up, my range just grew and I could hit it hard and strong. Discovering how I could do the whole death-metal voice was another end of the spectrum.

BILL: Do you notice any changes in your technique when you're singing the heavy growling stuff from when you're singing the regular stuff?

CHUCK: When I first started doing it, it was hurting my voice. I really noticed that, if I didn't do my vocal warm-ups and wasn't really ready to sing, I'd be hoarse the next day. I noticed I had to go through a routine to do it. So now, every time I sing, I have to go through this hour-long warm-up. It's a tape I got from Judy Davis. It's like a ritual now – if I don't do that tape, I have a hard time after the shows. If I do that tape, I never have a problem. When we did *Demonic*, which is really death-metal stuff, when we went on tour and I was singing that along with some of our old stuff, and I was having a hard time trying to do them both extreme, so I started breaking out the tapes and warming up a little more. It saw me through the end of the tour. A lot of the technique between the two styles is different. When I sing normally, I kind of pinch the vocals and close my throat down a little bit. When I sing the death stuff, I just open it up and push a lot of diaphragm.

BILL: So what do you think is producing the growl? What's the sensation in your mouth and throat when you growl?

CHUCK: It's more like from the gut.

BILL: Just more power, huh?

CHUCK: Yeah. Just the feeling of roaring like a lion. I can really hold it and control that stuff now. In the beginning, I never really sung a whole song like that; I just emphasised certain lines. Then, once death metal got a little more popular, I started experimenting with singing that way.

BILL: In the low and mid-range?

CHUCK: Yeah.

BILL: You don't use falsetto very often.

CHUCK: No. I used to, but after singing a lot of the harder heavy stuff, that falsetto range got lost. I still do screams, but those are more like a couple of words at a time. I don't do full songs in falsetto any more. That never really fit my style anyway. I was always more of a power singer. In the early days, with those Ratt-like bands, I didn't really fit in right because I was a big guy trying to sing powerful when it was supposed to be melodic stuff.

BILL: So are you a baritone, do you think?

CHUCK: Yeah.

BILL: Can you give me an idea of what your hour-long warm-up consists of?

CHUCK: It's just a lot of different scales and breathing exercises. Basically, after years of working with that tape, I've kind of converted it to my own style. A major part of my singing is having a lot of wind, so I do a lot of running and bicycling, just building up my lungs because without that I can't pull it off. So when I'm on the road, I do a lot of holding my breath. I just hold it for like two and a half, three minutes, just close eyes and hold it, go into another world. I also do a lot of humming, deep, deep humming where the voice vibrates. Once you get that sensation, like your nose starts tickling, you know it's starting to work.

On the road, that's how I gauge it. I've been doing this for so long now that, once my nose starts tickling, I know I'm ready to go. And I do a lot of mouth stretching and going through the vowels. And a couple of shots of Jack Daniel's doesn't hurt, either. I just try to get loose and be calm at the same time. I do the full tape, and afterward I just walk around humming real low notes.

BILL: You guys have done some extensive touring. To keep the voice strong, some singers do specific things like using a humidifier or drinking tea. What do you do on the road to keep your voice in shape?

CHUCK: I used to be like that, into humidifiers and tea, but I guess that, over time, you just find your own thing. It helps to go to the gym every day. I had a personal trainer out on the road, keeping us fit.

BILL: So a big part of it is being physically fit?

CHUCK: Yeah. Now, we don't party as hard as we used to, when we really needed [the gym]. We used to stay up drinking all night. Now, the show is what we're out there to do, so we hang out after the show, but we all get a good night's sleep. We take care of ourselves more, so we don't have to go to the gym. Like I said, I think we've found our routine that works for us.

In the early days, some tours involved playing like 35 shows in 32 days. That gets pretty brutal. It's all mental, where you get into a routine and stick to it.

BILL: Self-care is especially important in metal because it's harder on the voice than most other kinds of singing.

CHUCK: Right. I was on that death-vocal tour, and I was just like '[hoarse voice] Wow, man!' Right up to the last show, you're just barely making it. It's all mental. You might think, 'Man, can I do it?', and you get out there and there it is – the voice is there. Just go.

BILL: Have you ever damaged your voice?

CHUCK: Yeah, I did on the Clash Of The Titans tour in 1990 over in Europe. Of course, we weren't taking care of ourselves. I wasn't doing warm-ups, partying too much – all of those things combined and I hit a wall and lost my voice. I had laryngitis in Italy. I had to see a doctor, and he gave me cortisone shots to take with me. I had to inject myself with cortisone every night before I played, about 15 minutes before showtime. My voice would last me about an hour, and then after that it would be gone. I couldn't talk at all, so I'd have to go straight to bed. I couldn't talk for about a week. That was the most extreme injury I've had.

BILL: Have you ever hurt your voice trying to sing something that wasn't suited for you?

CHUCK: Not really, just that change from death-metal vocals to the other stuff. Before we wrote *Demonic*, I only had one death-metal song in the set. The following year, I had to sing six or seven songs like that within the set. That was the only time I thought, 'Man, I've got to figure this out or we've got to switch these songs and play something else.' I found that the vocal warm-ups were the biggest key. I'm just sold on it now. [Judy Davis] was great. She actually just passed away, but I've still got her tape and I live by that thing.

BILL: Do you pay any attention to breath support?

CHUCK: Well, my vocals are all built on taking in a lot of wind. I'm constantly huffing and puffing, trying to take in deep, deep loads of air.

BILL: If your voice gets tired during a performance, is the fatigue more in your throat or in your abdomen?

CHUCK: At the beginning of a tour, the first week, my stomach and diaphragm are sore because I'm not used to it. I mean, rehearsal is a lot different from going on-stage. The very first day, my throat is a little bit sore. But mostly it's the stomach muscles that get sore, just for about a week. You just gotta get over that hump. Once I'm over that, it's on.

But I take more care of myself now. I drink a metric shake when I come off-stage. I take vitamins before I go on-stage to keep me going. I take some energy pills before I go on. I never really lose energy on-stage. I usually get fired up, and when those pills kick in, I'm flying. And then I'm exhausted after; I'm drained. I'll drink a metric shake to replenish my body and then, you know, have a few beers. All those little tiny things you never think you'd do, you end up doing because, over the years, you realise they help. Before, I would just drink through the show – drink after, drink before – but it all catches up with you. You have to do those little things. It's like a ritual now. Every night before the show, everybody's doing the same things they did last night.

BILL: You've got more discipline in your approach than you had before.

CHUCK: Exactly. Once you figure out that it's not about you just having fun, it's about these people who pay to see you perform your best, because before, you'd be like, 'Here I am, I'm drunk, I'm having a good time,' and you'd do a shitty show. You're not up to par. You go away saying, 'Damn it, they didn't see me at my best.' Once we grew up and got serious about what we were doing out there, we wanted to give 100 per cent every night.

Wade Black

Wade sings for Seven Witches and is the former lead vocalist for Crimson Glory. A technically sound vocalist, Wade studied opera at the Bach Academy in Florida. He has a very high range, with the ability to sing soft ballads and screaming metal anthems.

BILL: What do you do to warm up, Wade?

WADE: What I usually do is kind of like a hum, kind of like keeping it in my head. And what I'll do is I'll go up and down my entire range – you know, kind of like 'Bbbbbbbbbb' with my lips. Humming's really good, too, as long as you have a bright resonating sound in your head. It's like when you're saying the word 'Nnnnnasty', you really get that coming out of the back of your throat. Like when you're talking across the room to somebody, you don't say, 'hey [softly]', you say, 'HEY!' – you definitely want to shoot it out there. That's what I usually do for my exercises to warm up.

BILL: You don't sing anything from the set to warm up?

WADE: No. I go out and at least get a good 45 minutes of getting everything warm, going through my scales, making sure my throat is clear. Your throat's like a muscle. Just jumping up there and doing it, you're looking for trouble. The warm-up is a must-have. Lots of water, too. Singing is all technique – it's not anything you can just go out there and do; it's definitely a learned thing.

BILL: Did you always have the range you've got now?

WADE: I have had quite a range. Actually, I would sing to the radio at a really young age. I've sung ever since I was four years old. I was in the elementary school choir. I've done plays here at the local playhouses also, and I've taken opera lessons from the same people that taught the Heart girls and Geoff Tate.

BILL: Who was that?

WADE: Dr John Barr. Actually, I was taught by one of his students that teaches down here in Florida. Same vocal system and lessons. When I was doing the opera lessons, that was at the Tampa Bay Performing Arts Center.

BILL: So you've had a lot of formal training?

WADE: Yeah, a lot.

BILL: More than the average heavy-metal singer?

WADE: I thought that, as far as doing the heavy music, you've definitely got to have some sort of training on technique. Support is definitely something you have to keep your mind on. You're breathing in through your nose. That way, you're setting up your diaphragm to work for you. As you breathe in, you can feel the diaphragm move, which is right under your rib cage.

A couple of months ago, my vocal coach told me I have to concentrate on my chest voice. There's a chest voice and a head voice. There are two gears that actually switch your voice. You know as well as I do, being a singer, that you're going to have your natural break in your voice. There's no quick cure for that; it's something you just have to muscle through, keep doing your lessons and keep on working. I mean, there was a pop in my voice to where it was like I had never sung before. It was terrible, going up mid into high range, but it's really natural for that to happen.

BILL: You also trained at the Bach Academy in Florida. Did you concentrate on opera there?

WADE: Yeah. The teacher, David Evans, sang professional opera for many, many years here and over in Europe. He actually wanted me to become a professional opera singer, but I don't think opera would have accepted a Mohawk at that time.

BILL: How do you reckon Pavarotti would do if he was asked to have a go at singing Crimson Glory?

WADE: I don't think he'd fare too well. Too many high notes! I don't think he'd be able to keep up. It's difficult stuff to have to sing. When Crimson Glory's album came out, I was called 'the second coming of Halford'. I was referenced to Tim 'Ripper' Owens all the time. What better people to be judged with than the people who are on top? But it's all about style. It's not about who's better than who. That's like saying that Geoff Tate is better than Rob Halford. They're both at the top of their game. It all comes down to style.

BILL: Do you have any personal horror stories about hurting your voice?

WADE: Actually, I had strep throat one time when I hadn't sung for a couple of months and I tried to sing. I've had a tonsillectomy and I've had cysts and ulcers on the back of my throat, probably from overworking and over-singing, or perhaps acid reflux.

I've sung so much at lessons, sometimes to the point that I end up being really hoarse, and I would ask my teacher about it and he would say, 'Oh, you're just not used to singing,' but I think that he just really overworked me and he wasn't correct in his teaching techniques. So you really have to watch out who you go to. It's good to find out who they've taught and who they've learned from.

To me, teaching is a different talent than singing. I don't think I have the tools to teach someone else how to sing. I can do it myself because of what I've read and what I've practised, but for me to teach somebody... I don't know if I could do it or not.

BILL: I think that's pretty common. It's the same way in sports. The great players, like Michael Jordan and Mario Lemieux, don't usually coach, and the mediocre players are often great coaches.

WADE: That might be true. It's a whole different skill.

BILL: Who influenced you?

WADE: I liked KISS, Foreigner, Iron Maiden, Creed, Rainbow. After I saw Maiden – my first show was Peace Of Mind – something broke inside of me. I mean, seeing that guy sing, somebody of that magnitude. From then on – maybe I was 16 or 17 years old – I really started to pursue the professional. I did my first gig when I was, like, 18.

BILL: Who's your favourite singer now?

WADE: It's hard to say. There are a lot of good singers out there. I like that guy that's in Live. He's got a really good voice. There aren't a lot of people that really grab me.

BILL: There isn't a lot of singing going on in much of the new rock.

WADE: No. The way that I always learned it, and the way that I always did it, was singing properly, enunciation and singing to where you could be heard, more so than all this death metal. All this growling, that does nothing but tear your throat up. You'll have no kind of singing career with that music. Pantera – I can't see how that guy can even speak, he's singing so hard. It's overkill.

BILL: So what about raspy singing?

WADE: If you have that natural effect to your voice to where you're able to do that and you're able to sing the next day, then you're able to do that. I think that comes with the part that you're God-given. I really don't have a lot of gruff to my voice. If I do, I have more of a tendency to push a little bit harder to get that gruffy sound.

BILL: I was listening to the song 'War Of The Worlds'. There's a pretty high note in the beginning, and it's kind of rough, edgy.

WADE: It does have a little bit of a gruff to it, I guess. Maybe that's something you learn over time. It's kind of like when you listen to Eric Clapton sing, that little bit of gruff that he does - that's what gets him through his mid-range. He really doesn't have a full-range singing voice.

And also, if you see Geoff Tate sing, or somebody of that magnitude, you can always tell where their breaking point is. Even Rob Halford has it. You know, he's got probably the best voice I've ever heard for that style of music. His mid-range is just... I don't think that there's a note that he can't get. I think he's got the perfect voice.

BILL: So, for you, does your technique differ when singing clean from singing with a growl?

WADE: Yeah, it does. When I'm singing clean, I'm more concentrating on my support, my opening of the back of my throat, which I think is really important. The opening in the back of the throat needs to be wide. That way, you're giving yourself room enough to do what you need to do. When you're singing gruff, I think you're tending to close up your throat a little bit. Your vocal cords are just going crazy. It's not good for you. It's over-extending your voice. It's like going to a football game and screaming your head off and then not being able to talk for a couple of days. It's like blowing through a blade of grass between your two fingers - the edges of your vocal cords get all chafed, like your lips.

You have to take care of yourself. Rest, water, practice, technique and so on – over and over again. It really sounds boring. You're doing your lessons and saying, 'Man, I want to switch from that first tape all the way to number ten. I want to learn how to scream!' I was the same way. I wanted to rush all that, but there was no rushing it because I kept on trying to do it the wrong way and kept on getting more hoarse and probably set myself behind. The practice part – it has to take place. There's no way around it.

BILL: Are there any resonating sensations you feel?

WADE: When I'm singing in my lower to mid range, I've got a lot of chest buzz, a good feeling there in the chest - a nice steady tone you work with first, then you try go for your range. But you get that bright Frank Sinatra tone in the mask part of your face. You want to sing like you're projecting out of the top of your head, almost. As I'm going up my scale, I can hear it more so resonating in my sinuses.

BILL: When you go into the head voice, there's still a lot of force there, right?

WADE: Oh, yeah. Head voice is just your falsetto voice strengthened to a full voice. It doesn't happen on every note - you have your physical limit - but I can go ahead and go all the way up and all the way down without any breaks or anything in there. It's been almost 14 years that I've been doing this. But what's really funny is that it's only been in the last five or six that I've really taken it seriously. So think of what I would have been able to do if I had been able to really grasp it earlier more so than trying to do what I wanted to do instead of what I was supposed to do.

BILL: Do you tend to sing loudly or at a conversational level?

WADE: I really don't think that you should ever sing any louder than you talk with your normal voice. You need to use your microphone and let the PA work for you. You've definitely got to be able to hear yourself in some sort of monitor system. If not, you're just fighting against yourself. What I'll do a lot of times is I'll go ahead and plug one of my ears off, totally, with earplugs or whatever. That way, you're hearing the voice in your head. You always see the professional singers when they're on-stage - they put their hand over their ear because they can't hear. A lot of people will have those wireless monitors in their ear so they can hear themselves. Most of the time, any singers that are on-stage and don't have any monitors, they're over-singing. They're not going to be singing the next night.

BILL: So you never sing really loud?

WADE: You shouldn't have to. It actually seems like you're getting louder, but you're not. It's just the pitch change as you're going up. But I think, if you're going to sing high, definitely keep it in your head. If it hurts in your throat, go back and redo your lessons because you're doing something wrong. There shouldn't be any tension in your throat whatsoever. Your jaw - let it just hang down. Do your vowels and really enunciate. Learning to pay attention to all that stuff takes time. It's all in the practice, even though it sounds boring. But nothing beats experience, getting out there and trying a few things. I go out with my friends and sing karaoke, just for kicks. I love it. For beginning singers, maybe that's a starting point.

BILL: How do you improvise on a bad-singing day?

WADE: This is going to be bad news for everybody: there is no improvising on a bad day. If you sing with a cold or strep throat and your voice starts to break up and you get hoarse and you keep singing, you just mess yourself up even worse. You'd like to say there's a singer's secret – teas and honey – but I've tried everything and there's nothing that's going to save you from a cold.

BILL: What if you're on-stage and you're tired?

WADE: Well, you've heard some of the old Crimson Glory stuff. I had to cover some of that. This guy, when he sings high, all the dogs start howling. I had to do a lot of that stuff, and it all depends on how good a shape you're in, how much practice time you get every day.

Stamina was a problem for me. I thought I was going to have to problem over in Europe because I started doing my fourth and fifth night in a row. But when you want it bad enough, you definitely push yourself to keep into shape. In the studio, I had pre-recorded background vocals on the chorus to reinforce that, because there's no way I'm going to go out and sing 'War Of The Worlds' or a song like that and expect to do that every night. It's humanly impossible – unless you're Rob Halford. If you're Rob Halford you can go out and pretty much do whatever you want.

BILL: What do you do to keep your stamina during touring?

WADE: Gotta keep singing. When I didn't think I was going to make it to that third or fourth night, I was humming all day, everywhere.

BILL: So you'd vocalise all day? You wouldn't take it easy and not speak?

WADE: No, no. I've heard that - don't talk, be quiet - but the more you use your voice correctly, the more it's going to strengthen. Unless you're sick or your throat hurts, go about your normal life. But if you've sung for the last four nights and you're kind of scared about what you're going to sound like, maybe it is a good idea to back off a little bit and bring your bag of magic out, whatever it calls for that night.

BILL: Do you practise differently when you're home?

WADE: Not at all. I still practise to the radio. I come in here, put my headphones on and just scream until the neighbours bang on the door. When we're practising in the warehouses, I tend to pay more attention to how I sound, but my overall voice is still there pretty much every day. But you've got to know how to get there before you can get there.

BILL: Is rock singing more difficult than other styles?

WADE: Absolutely. Rock singing is like your power vocals. Look at Steven Tyler - now there's a rock 'n' roll singer! Ian Gillian, David Coverdale, Robert Plant - those are rock singers because it's a power vocal. Even myself: power vocals. Chris Cornell: power vocals.

BILL: In contrast to a band like Journey, for instance.

WADE: Yes, that's definitely not rock. That's pop. Technically, Steve Perry is probably one of the best singers that there is, but I don't think that he has too many different faces to his voice. When you hear Ripper do his stuff... I mean that kid's got the whole package.

BILL: Do you think good singing is more about talent, work or technique?

WADE: I think that the practice part, no matter how good you think you are, is always going to make you better. If I didn't sing for a couple of months and tried to go on-stage – it doesn't happen like that. It's a muscle. If you don't exercise muscle, you get out of shape. Innate talent overrides any of those other things. You still have to practise. Technique is a major thing. It's the prowess of everything that singing is about. It's not how hard you push; it's how much you need to get that steady tone. Then go from there.

Corey Brown

Corey, lead singer of Magnitude 9 and formerly of Psycho Drama, is one of the finest melodic vocalists in progressive metal, with a voice that has been compared to Don Dokken and Rik Emmett.

BILL: When I first heard a clip of your singing on the Internet, I knew right away that I wanted you in this book. Your voice is very clean and smooth.

COREY: Well, thanks. I'm honoured to do it.

BILL: Have you ever taken any vocal lessons?

COREY: I haven't taken any one-on-one vocal training, like with a vocal coach. I probably should, but I've been doing it for so long now that I've probably developed some nasty habits that I don't want to change. I started singing when I was three or four years old. Actually, I didn't sing in junior high and high school because I was a drummer in a jazz band. I played drums for seven years. Eventually, I was doing the Don Henley thing: singing behind the kit.

BILL: That's hard to do.

COREY: Yeah. It got to the point where every time we tried out a vocalist, I would sing it better than he would, so I decided to try to find a drummer to replace me so I could just sing. I like drumming, but I liked being up front more. I purchased a couple of vocal training books and cassettes. I got Jim Gillette's tapes. He used to sing for a glam band. It's ironic because I always though he was a hokey singer, but those are probably the most helpful tapes I've ever purchased. They were just teaching rudimentary things, like scales to a piano. Every night on the way to rehearsal I used to throw in the cassette and practise the piano scales.

BILL: Are you a tenor?

COREY: I couldn't even tell you. There's that classic joke: 'You should sing tenor.' And the guy goes, 'Oh yeah?' 'Yeah, 10 or 15 miles from here because you're driving me nuts.' I'd probably say I'm a tenor.

BILL: You've been singing for a long time. Who inspired you?

COREY: It was 1983. I was sitting in an art class in junior high school. This kid let me hear this band called Queensrÿche. At the time, I was listening to stuff like Van Halen, Journey, Metallica and Dio. I heard 'Take Hold Of The Flame', and I was mesmerised by Geoff Tate. It was pretty much him and Bruce Dickinson that were my primary inspirations. Bruce is such a powerful vocalist. He's got the range but he's also got that raw power, whereas Geoff capitalises on the high, melodic vocals. A lot of people say I kind of sound like Geoff Tate, although I don't deliberately try to. I guess it's just the way I've trained myself to sing.

BILL: How do you warm up for a show?

COREY: I used to be very into Dream Theater and Queensrÿche, so I was always trying to sing dynamically and have soaring high vocals and crystal-clear vocals. I went through several different phases where I relied on several tricks of the trade I'd read about. There were several voodoo things I had to do before a show, like I had to gargle with salt water, and I had to have warm tea with honey in it. I used to scale up and down for about 15 minutes before I got on-stage. One time, I did so many scales that I stretched out my vocal cords before I even got on the stage.

BILL: You blew out your voice?

COREY: It was there but I was straining to get it to go. It's my personal belief that it's 95 per cent attitude and five per cent technique. Once you establish your technique, no matter how experienced you are, if you convince yourself that you can do it, you will. Now, pretty much what I do is I don't drink and I don't smoke. I occasionally drink a beer, but that's about it. I try to keep plenty of fluids going through me. I'm kind of a hypochondriac. Every time my nose starts to run, I think, 'I'd better go get some medicine.'

BILL: Do you sleep with a humidifier?

COREY: I used to. Here in Colorado it's really dry, especially in the winter, and we're in the high altitude, so there are times I've slept with a humidifier. We're about 7,000 feet above sea level, and I see a lot of vocalists get winded when they come up here. It's a benefit to me because, when we recorded in Los Angeles, I could sing for ten hours in the studio with no trouble, then I'd wake up the next morning and sing for another ten hours.

BILL: As far as practice goes, you don't do scales any more?

COREY: I do a lot of mouth stretches because my jaw tends to get stiff on me. I guess it's a product of what they call TMJ [Temporomandibular Joint Disorder], which is almost like arthritis of the jaw. If you're singer, you don't want to have that. But I had a very mild case of it. So I do mouth stretches and exercises, 'Ah, ay, ee, oh, oo.' I'll do some humming exercises, going up the scale. It's about a 20-minute drive to rehearsal, so I'm usually ready by the time I get there.

I used to go through some serious warm-up exercises, but I got to a point where I would over-exert my voice just trying to get it ready to go. It's funny because I was at a local show one night and I saw Seventh Sign. The vocalist [Gregg Analla] was awesome. He reminded me of Ray Alder. I asked him, 'What do you do before you come on?' He said, 'Well, I don't do scales because usually it burns me out before I get on-stage, so I just hum a bit, do some body stretches and go though this mental game of telling myself I'm gonna hit all the notes. Then I sing and I'm fine.' So I tried it and it worked.

BILL: Suppose you have no shows scheduled. I'm sure you don't go long periods without singing, right?

COREY: Right. The longest I've gone without singing is three weeks, and of course then I try to ease into it. It's like running – if you haven't done it for a while, you don't want to start right into a full sprint. But yeah, I just do the classic scales. There's 'ma, me, may, mo, moo' and 'do, re, mi, fa, so, la, ti, do' – All the ones you saw in Bugs Bunny as a kid. I do that kind of stuff, but I don't do it like I used to. I used to do 20 minutes of scales and then I'd get to rehearsal and I'd be burned out.

For me, the warm-up is more of a mental psych-out thing than a physical thing. I used to get so freaked out before a show that I was going to crack or I wouldn't be able to scream, and sometimes I wouldn't, so after a while I just started thinking, 'Okay, it's just a show. I've proven myself. I can do this.' And I still get nervous before a show, but usually we schedule the first couple of songs as something that's comfortable in my range, that I can warm up to.

BILL: Have you ever just frozen up playing live?

COREY: Yeah, I've cracked. I've popped. I've had a couple of times where I hit the first note and it panicked me, like an ice skater – they miss the first jump and their whole routine is thrown off. I had to re-evaluate what was going on. I had some really high notes and expectations. The audience was expecting to hear the album and I didn't hit it. It was very disappointing. But they didn't boo me off the stage or anything. I think the toughest time has been while I was sick. Especially as a vocalist, if you've got some kind of sinus-related problem, it creates difficulty in breathing. The way the tones resonate through your head is completely different. The way you hear things is completely different. I would say a cold is a singer's worst nightmare. That and strep throat.

BILL: When you're singing, do you consciously think of breath support?

COREY: Yeah. I do goofy little exercises sometimes when I'm sitting around or on the way somewhere. I'll take a deep breath and count out loud as far as I can before I run out of breath. That's a good exercise for the diaphragm. When I first started singing, I used to lay on my back and put a couple of books on my stomach and try to inhale and raise the books, then exhale and watch the books fall. Before I sing, I do a lot of stretches, like touch my toes.

Posture's important, too. Even standing at a slight arch, or bowing a little bit, you start to cramp the freedom of your diaphragm, so one thing I don't do before a show is eat a heavy meal. If you do, you don't really have room to expand the diaphragm. There have been times when I went on while I was really hungry. I might eat a banana or something, but I'd rather have that freedom of movement in the diaphragm area. And I don't wear anything constrictive around my waist. Breath support is 90 per cent of it. If you're tired and you're not breathing correctly, you're not going to hit your notes. If you don't deliver enough breath, you'll start singing from your throat.

BILL: And breath support is key in sustaining notes.

COREY: Oh, absolutely. Sometimes, while we're practising, I'll just randomly grab a note and carry it, just to see how long I can go with it. The guys look at me like I'm a nut.

BILL: For you, what is the key to singing long phrases?

COREY: I visualise it like a ski jumper. You've gotta prepare before you hit the jump, make sure that you're allowing yourself the time to take the proper breath before you deliver that note. You'll know if you hit it right because you'll feel it coming from the diaphragm and resonating in the head. If you don't hit it right, you'll feel it coming from your chest and resonating through your throat, and usually you cut out quick. You can't hold it as long. That's what's always impressed me about Bruce Dickinson. He just grabs it and 'Ahhhhhhh!' Twenty minutes later, you're looking for Bugs Bunny's glove shaking in the air. Another key to hitting a long note is giving yourself a little vibrato. Vibrato seems to allow you to carry the notes longer because you're dissipating the air, cutting it in and out, so I use a lot of vibrato because I can sustain my notes longer that way. Plus, I think it sounds better.

BILL: Sometimes on sustained notes, it can feel like you're just singing on a thread of air, almost like you're sucking the air back in. Have you ever had that sensation?

COREY: Yeah. I've held notes so long that I get light-headed. It's a light-headedness that almost feels like air's coming back in through your nose as you're still exhaling it. It's like a vacuum. Yeah, I've experienced that before. I think the basic foundation of being a vocalist is to first establish the correct method of breathing. The first thing I learned to develop, when I was like 14 years old, was learning to take a breath without raising my shoulders. I'd fold a piece of paper in half and I would stand it up across the kitchen table from me, and I would practise taking a deep breath and trying to blow it over. So if I blew it over at two feet, I would slide it back another foot, and so on, until I couldn't blow it over any more. Or if the paper was too light I would move on to something heavier, like a piece of cardboard. When paper got boring, I would work with a candle, trying to blow the flame out. It sounds really hokey, but it worked.

BILL: On a deep breath, do you feel it in your lower back?

COREY: Yeah, you can feel your back expand. I've been doing it so long now, it's kind of an unconscious thing.

BILL: It's a sensation for people to use so they know they're getting it right?

COREY: Oh, yeah. You know, I think teaching vocals would be the most frustrating thing. If you're learning to play guitar, you say, 'Here's where your fingers go on the strings.' Or if you're learning to play drums, 'This is how you hold the sticks.' But to learn to sing, it's so internally mechanical that there's no way you can say to your students, 'Okay, this is the proper way to deliver it.' The only thing you can see physically is whether or not they're breathing correctly.

Another good technique to practise, to make sure your breaths are being properly delivered, at least for me, was I would put my index finger on my

Adam's apple. As you're changing pitch, you can tend to feel your Adam's apple rise and fall. If you're delivering the correct amount of air, you shouldn't feel it rise or fall very much. The Adam's apple should never rise clear up into your chin. If it does, you're not delivering the correct amount of air and you're singing from your throat instead of your diaphragm.

BILL: Do you find that your larynx pretty much stays the same?

COREY: Yeah.

BILL: Even on very high notes?

COREY: It depends. If I'm singing in a head voice, it'll stay pretty much in the same area. If I move into falsetto, I can feel it rise up. One of the most difficult tasks for me as a singer was to make the screams blend from the head voice to a falsetto and still sound powerful without having a departure between the two notes. You don't want to go 'Ahhhh-ahhhh [rising note that breaks into falsetto]'; you want 'Ahhhhhhhhhhhhhhhhhh [rising note with no break]'.

BILL: You want the same tone all the way up.

COREY: Yeah. And that's just technique, really. The more I worked on it, the better I got. When I first started, I felt like a 13-year-old kid, like 'Ah-ah-ah-ah-ah [breaking in and out of falsetto]'. One of the books I read recommended that you do your scales saying, 'Nay.' That's a good way to practise going from head voice to falsetto.

BILL: Because that's an easier vowel?

COREY: Yeah. 'Eees' are the toughest for me. But 'eees' will help you develop breath delivery because when you're going high 'eee' it gets tough. 'Ah' and 'nay' are good warm-up scales for me. If I've had a hard singing day and the next day I have to do it again, I'll practise going 'ah-ah-ah-ah-ah-ah-ah [ascending scale, the fourth note being the highest, then descending]'. Sometimes I'll just idle 'ahhhhhhhhhhhh [mid-low rumbling note]'.

BILL: You're relaxed with 'ahh,' while with 'eee' you have to tense things?

COREY: 'Eee' is tough. It's for when you really want to push it.

BILL: It's strange, because some vocalists still sound great even though their larynx shoots way up under their chin.

79

COREY: Yeah, some people are naturally gifted. Anyone can learn to sing, but not everyone can sing well. The physical structure is important.

BILL: When going through the break, what sensations do you feel in your throat or mouth as you try to keep the note full?

COREY: Head voice, to me, has always been about feeling the air flowing through your cheekbones and nose.

BILL: You feel the resonation there?

COREY: Yeah. But you have to deliver more air to keep it there. If you let up, it's gonna come right through your throat and mouth. So it's almost like the same way you feel when you're trying to inflate a balloon – you feel the air through your cheekbones and nose. There are times I've felt my teeth resonate.

BILL: The back teeth?

COREY: Top, front. That's how I know I'm hitting it right, if I can feel the top bridge of my mouth and my front teeth and my nasal passage. If I can feel all those resonate together, I know I'm hitting it just perfect.

BILL: And the resonation changes on different vowels and different pitches.

COREY: Yeah.

BILL: Do you have a break in your voice any more?

COREY: There's a slight departure.

BILL: There's a certain placement that some people use to get through the break, such as biting down on the note.

COREY: Yeah. For me, I try to deliver more air through the transition and then less air once I get up there. If I deliver too much air in falsetto, I blow it out. You lose the note and go flat or sharp, and you'll have a tendency to crack.

BILL: How about growling?

COREY: It was a very unnatural feeling at first.

BILL: You're talking about the low-range growling?

COREY: Yeah. It took a while to develop it to the point where I was comfortable with it. I had a tendency to growl too much and blow my voice out, or make the notes sound garbled. So I never growled very much. I put a little bit of gravel in there every now and then. Growing up, I used to screw around with impersonations. Trying to emulate other characters' sounds, you learn to utilise your vocal cords in different ways. You know, like, 'Rootin, tootin, rascally rabbit! [Yosemite Sam voice]' is almost the same as singing, 'Yeahhhh [growling tone].' It's basically the same technique.

For me, growling is definitely from the throat, which is an unnatural feeling when all you've done is worked at singing through your nose. So I like to do it for power, but I try not to overdo it. As for growling in a high-pitched scream, when you're in falsetto and you're growling, that's even tougher. I couldn't even describe how to do it, but I can feel it when it's right.

BILL: Are you a loud singer?

COREY: If I'm in the head voice, I'm loud. If I'm singing falsetto, I'm softer. But I don't push a whole lot more air when singing than I do when I'm talking.

BILL: So you don't take big, deep breaths during a song?

COREY: Not unless I'm doing a really long line or something really powerful that's got to sustain for a long time. If you take too big of a breath you'll throw it flat or sharp. I've worked for 15 years on technique, and now I can actually sing and have fun with it. For a lot of years, it was really frustrating – I tried desperately to hit the high notes and be really powerful, but the harder I tried, the worse I got. It's like throwing darts: if you're really concentrating on the bullseye, you seem to do worse than if you just get up there and throw the dart.

BILL: Has your range increased or has it always been the same?

COREY: It's definitely increased. I listen to tapes of me from 1990 and I hear notes that I used to struggle with, that I could barely hit, and now they're like a cakewalk. Even on a night that I'm not warmed up, I could easily hit those notes. It's like with anything: the more you practise, the better you get. If I were to stop singing altogether and try to sing a year from now, I'd have difficulty hitting notes. Even if we re-introduce a song that we dropped a year ago, I sometimes have difficulty hitting the high notes.

BILL: Have you ever damaged your voice?

COREY: Nothing severe. I've had a couple of experiences where my range was limited because we over-practised in the days before a show and it took more effort than normal to get my voice limber enough to hit those notes again that night of the show. Since that experience, I never try to over-extend my voice the night before a show; I just do what it takes to get through the song. But I've never damaged it to where I woke up and couldn't speak or anything.

BILL: Are you a perfectionist?

COREY: Yes! I'm a perfectionist and a hypochondriac. If I'm gonna be in the studio tonight, I'm waking up in the morning going, 'Okay, how's the sinuses? How's the throat feel? Did I drink enough water last night?' I try to avoid caffeine because it tends to make the muscles tense and atrophies them. The most important thing for me is sleep. People are like, 'Why are you so concerned about getting sick?' But when your body is your instrument, you've got to be concerned. There have been times before a show when I'm feeling sick and the guys are like, 'What are you so freaked about?' and I'm like, 'Hey, if you had to play guitar with a glove on your hand, you'd probably be disappointed, too.'

BILL: Like, if you're a guitarist, you don't want to get into fistfights.

COREY: Exactly. If you're a guitarist, you're gonna protect your hands. But I try to be a little more laid back now. I've tried to develop an attitude of 'Well, you know the voice is always going to be there.' For the longest time, it was almost a voodoo thing: 'Okay, tonight I'm gonna sip some tea and I'm gonna do scales. I hope my voice is as powerful as it was last night.'

BILL: Even so, sometimes the voice just isn't there, no matter what you do.

COREY: Right. I've experienced that myself and I don't even know how to explain it. A lot of it is about mental preparation. What's going on in your life definitely makes a difference. If you're having a lot of stress or you're fatigued, that's gonna play a part. It kind of sucks being a singer. Well, I guess all the parts that are cool even out with all the parts that suck [laughs].

BILL: Do you ever sing karaoke?

COREY: Yeah. I like to do that song 'Babe' by Styx. I'll be sitting in the karaoke room and all these people are shit-faced, and they're singing the best they can and I'll get up there out of the blue and the piano starts playing and I start singing, 'Babe, I'm leaving, I must be on my way,' and people's jaws are hitting tables. They're like, 'Dude, it's Dennis DeYoung!' It's just fun. For one thing, you get to do something different. I mean, I've even done Michael Jackson. It's good exercise for the voice – and for the ego.

John Bush

John has a distinct, gravelly vocal style that he has mastered over his 20-year career. He is best known for his work with two renowned metal bands: Armored Saint and Anthrax. He is a charismatic and energetic frontman.

BILL: How did you get started singing?

JOHN: A friend of mine was putting a talent show together in junior high school. I was about 13 and we were all totally into music. However, I didn't have any knowledge that I was going to be doing anything with it – I maybe played some air guitar on a tennis racket or something, as everybody does – but he asked me if I wanted to sing in this band. I said, 'Why me? I've never thought about singing.' His philosophy was that I had a big mouth and I was kind of popular, so therefore I was just a role model of a lead singer, so we did it and it went over big. It just opened up a new door.

As time went on, I tried to pursue it seriously and dedicate myself to improving. By the time high school ended and Armored Saint was getting started, I seemed to find a sound of my own, just a little scratchy thing that has gone on to be kinda my trademark.

BILL: Did you take lessons at any point?

JOHN: Yeah, a bunch of times. The first one, I can't remember his name now, but I remember that every time I walked in his house it smelled like cat piss so bad. It sucked! It was hard to open my mouth to even attempt to sing.

BILL: Was he telling you to take a lot of deep breaths?

JOHN: Exactly! Then, in '83 or '84, I took lessons from a teacher named Elizabeth Barron. She was cool. She taught me exercises that I still use to this day.

BILL: Is that what you do to warm up for a show?

JOHN: Yeah. And I just learned a new one taught to me by Jeff Duncan, who plays in Armored Saint with me. It's similar to doing a stretching routine before playing an athletic event. I'm always open to learning things. It's funny because one time Sebastian Bach heard me warming up and he suggested a different time to warm up. He's like, 'You're doing it too soon before the show. Why don't you try an hour before the show and then do it again ten minutes before the show?'

BILL: When were you doing it?

JOHN: I was doing it half an hour before the show. So I've changed the intervals now, and it seems to work. I'm pretty serious about it, even though it gets old. Everybody in the band is like, 'Here he goes again.' Believe me, I hate doing it, too. It keeps you loose and warmed up. It's kind of like my security blanket. So I do this new warm-up now that sounds like this: 'Ahh-ahhh [sings two notes a fifth apart].' It's a good warm-up. Big intervals.

BILL: Do you ascend the scale with that?

JOHN: Yeah, you just go up the scale. And that one will really let you know where you stand, as far as warming up goes. To me, the warm-up is just a way to save my voice. If you go out there cold and just start screaming, which I do sometimes, you're just gonna blow it out. It's a way to get your voice to a gradual adjustment.

BILL: Have you ever ended up damaging your voice?

JOHN: I've hurt my voice a couple times. I hurt it one time when Anthrax was on tour with Pantera. That alone is enough, just the debauchery that takes place when touring with Pantera... I ended up getting an infection in my throat. I wasn't aware of it; I just knew that, at the end of the tour, I was really shot. And we were only doing an opening set. I took off about a week. Then we were getting ready to record, and when I came into the studio I just couldn't do it. My voice was hurting and it was not hitting registers. I was freaking out, like, 'Oh my god, I'm losing my voice.'

I went to see a throat specialist. There are two doctors that I see, depending on what coast I'm on. One's in LA. His name is Dr Joseph Sugarman, who everybody sees, whether it's pop stars, hard rock stars, actors – everybody. He's awesome. Then there's another doctor on the East Coast who is his liaison, named Dr Kessler. I went to go see him because I was in New York. It turned out I had two infections in my throat. Not just one, two! Plus, it was swollen as hell. That was somewhat comforting to me because I knew it wasn't just a mental thing.

BILL: And it wasn't permanent.

JOHN: Right. That's the important thing. The doctor ended up giving me this cortisone, which they're reluctant to do, but I've done it a couple times when my vocal cords were just totally swollen. I ended up taking a bunch of medication for the infection as well. He goes, 'Rest for ten days. Don't do anything. Don't even speak.'

It was pretty difficult. And he put me on this gnarly diet, because these guys really believe that certain foods that you eat have a lot to do with it. Acid reflux splashes on the back of your vocal cords and really messes with your vocal cords badly, so he put me on this particular medication to prevent acid reflux, and I couldn't eat spicy foods. Then, as soon as I started singing again, it was like I could knock walls down with my voice. It was pretty amazing.

BILL: Some singers are pretty careful about taking care of their voice on the road. Do you do things like drink tea and have a humidifier in the room?

JOHN: I kind of teeter on this tightrope. I know I need to take care of myself, especially now because I'm 38 years old. You can't bounce back from anything. Getting a hangover is harder to deal with. But I also don't want to baby my voice because you become a hypochondriac. I don't want to live like that.

It's a fine line. I always try to monitor how much I drink. I used to make sure that, if I had been out partying, I always had an off day the next day. Obviously, that's changed a little bit lately. I find that, for me, anyway, if I have a couple shots of whiskey or something, I'm a little bit more uninhibited as a performer. It brings out a little bit more of a spontaneous side to my stage persona, and I like that. I don't think I'm a perfect singer by any means. My whole thing lies more in attitude and coming off as a great frontman.

BILL: Do you drink a lot of water?

JOHN: I drink a *lot* of water! Water is really important for me. I personally hate tea. I'm a coffee guy. I associate tea with a medicinal purpose. I'll definitely drink herbal tea if my throat is hurting, but if I don't have to, I won't. I like coffee. In fact, I'm pouring myself a cup right now [laughs]. Another problem I have – and Dr Sugarman told me this – is I have a tendency to talk really loud. Every time we get on the phone, he's like, 'John, quiet down.'

BILL: You're a high-energy guy!

JOHN: Exactly.

BILL: Does it ever wear your voice out?

JOHN: Sure. Talking is one of the worst things. I've heard that Sting will not say a word before a show. Even Celine Dion, who, even though I despise her music, is an amazing singer - she won't talk at all. She'll write notes. To me, that's a little too much, but I'm sure it does help her voice out.

BILL: Do you sing at a loud volume, too?

JOHN: I do. I really try to be conscientious of that because you really don't have to sing loud. You've got the amplification. Armored Saint just did a tour with Dio — the guy's phenomenal. He's amazing. And the funny thing is, he doesn't project that hard live. That's probably why he's saved his voice all these years.

BILL: You've gotta let the mic do the work, huh?

JOHN: You do. And let the soundman help you. One major problem is if you don't have good monitors, which happens sometimes if you're just opening up for someone or doing a festival. That's where you might start over-compensating because you're not hearing yourself. Plus, adrenaline kicks in and makes you want to scream and go nuts, but you have to try to find a way to not do that. I have a problem sometimes with that because I'm an over-zealous kind of guy.

BILL: Has your range increased over the years?

JOHN: It's probably decreased. That's something that happens when you get older. But I think I'm a better singer now. I'm more in touch with my style and persona. To me, my goal has always been to have a unique voice, so people say, 'Yeah, I know that guy's voice. That guy sounds cool.' So it's gotten deeper. I'm sure alcohol has had a lot to do with that. But I think I'm ballsier than ever and have more command of my voice.

BILL: Do you think that it's important for aspiring singers to find their own unique voice?

JOHN: I think it is. All of my favourite singers are ones that are really distinctive. Bon Scott, I think he's a really amazing singer. He wasn't too concerned about his range and all that; it was just about the sound and the identity. The same goes for Dio, who is probably a better singer than Bon

Scott was. Rob Halford – a phenomenal singer but also very distinctive. Or Phil Mogg, who was a hero of mine – you heard the voice and you knew immediately who it was. That's something that's driven me.

BILL: Is there a different technique when you sing with a growl compared to when you sing clean?

JOHN: You can do it without blowing your voice out. You know who's an amazing singer, strangely enough, is Chris Barnes from Six Feet Under. For that guy to be able to do that death-metal voice, it's like, 'How does he do it?' If I did that, within ten seconds I'd be hoarse. How he pulls that off, I'm not quite sure. I don't think that he projects that hard, so maybe that's how he's able to do it.

BILL: Do you pay any attention to breath support when you're singing?

JOHN: Well, when you're doing some screaming and belting, you're gonna be using your throat. My teacher at one point said, 'Rod Stewart is a terrible singer.' I remember thinking to myself, 'He may be terrible, but he's Rod Stewart! That guy's had an enormous career out of that voice of his.'

Joacim Cans

Since 1996, when Joacim became lead singer of Hammerfall, the band has seen tremendous success. They have topped the Swedish album sales charts and been nominated for a Swedish Grammy. Joacim has a clean, melodic vocal style.

BILL: How loudly do you sing?

JOACIM: I guess it all depends on what style I'm singing. As a metal vocalist there's a lot of power involved when I sing compared to the more laid-back style of musicals.

BILL: Do you sing as loudly in the studio as you do on-stage?

JOACIM: In the studio, my technique is much better, and when everything works I can use my resonance chambers better to get a fuller vocal production. On-stage, you're so into your stage presence, so I tend to be much louder compared to the studio.

BILL: Does your volume tend to increase as you go up the range?

JOACIM: Not really, but I bring a lot of power into my falsetto and maybe that creates more volume in the end, especially when I sing live. In the studio I use my resonance chambers more as I climb up the range scale.

BILL: Does your technique change as you go up the range – for example, open throat, more power from the abdomen?

JOACIM: When I go up the range, I try not to push too hard. That can kill your cords. An open throat and feeling the 'cold spot' in the back of your mouth cavity, behind the hard palate, makes it easier to get the high notes. Also, singing on the tail end of the breath works for me. One important thing is that the higher you go, the lesser the airflow, compared to the deep chest, voice where the airflow is much more intense.

BILL: On high notes, what sensations do you feel in your head?

JOACIM: When I hit a high note properly, it feels like my head is one huge resonance chamber, like a big cathedral or something like that. It's a great sensation when it finally works. When it doesn't work, my whole body gets tense, which it makes it hard to sing anything high at all.

BILL: How do you manage the register change from chest to head voice?

JOACIM: I'm taught that you use both registers whenever you sing in your head or chest voice. Otherwise you get that awful crack when going from chest to head voice. I'm just bringing some head voice down to the chest, and as I climb up, the head voice takes over more and more, but never without losing the chest voice.

BILL: Did you always have the range you have now?

JOACIM: I guess I had to work really hard to get my head voice going. My mid-range has always been strong, and I try to do most of my singing in that range. When I started out as a singer, my falsetto was not there at all. That made my skills as a vocalist very limited. The best thing to do while developing your high range, as well as the real deep voice, is to isolate the falsetto. That's what I did, and it really helped me gain a lot of range. It's pretty simple to do this. You just have to find your 'child' voice and do exercises using that voice.

BILL: How does your technique differ when singing high notes clean versus singing them with an edge? Is there more throat constriction, more push from the abdomen and so on?

JOACIM: I must say that I have never been into the growling type of vocals, putting an edge to my voice. When I started out as a singer, my vocal gurus were the ones using their voices in a natural way, without modifying them in any way. I have always tried to get a voice as clean as possible, to stay true to the voice I was born with and the voice that makes me unique. It's a whole different way of singing – adding an edge to it. Some people have learned singing that way and can barely take a clean note and keep it without making it flat or sharp.

If I add too much edge to my voice I wouldn't last one song. I would strain my voice and become hoarse for the next week. The only place I try to add edge is in my lower range. The technique is the same but the expressions are different. I guess the face changes when you add edge to the singing, and the facial muscles get tense. When you find the right sensation, you'll find that it doesn't take much effort to get a great voice with a nice edge to it. Never push too hard! The important thing is to remain relaxed in the throat and body because, if you get tense in your throat, you can ruin your voice.

BILL: When singing, do you pay any special attention to breath support?

JOACIM: Breathing is something we do as a reflex, and we shouldn't emphasise too much on that matter. As long as you have a natural airflow and a natural breathing, you should think about the placement instead. Never take a deep breath before you take a high note! Never 'get ready' for the killer note; just let your vocal cords do the job. They create the tones, the breathing doesn't.

BILL: How do you improvise when you're having a bad-singing day?

JOACIM: The most important thing is trying not to push and force the voice out of your mouth. After you have done your warm-ups, you should know what's going on with your voice. I always take it easy in the first part of the show, skipping the really high notes and replacing them with lower harmonies, transposing an octave or letting the audience sing instead. If you push it too hard, you'll get a nice little hangover the next day and your voice will be in an even worse shape. Always listen to your body!

BILL: What burns your voice out the most when singing?

JOACIM: Songs that are in a key not suitable for me, especially when there are many parts of really high-pitched vocals following each other. Another thing is the environment: a hall with a lot of smoke can really ruin my voice, as can too many pyrotechnics, including a lot of gunpowder smoke and halls without air conditioning. In all these cases, drinking water – not too cold – is the best way to keep your cords lubricated.

BILL: If you get tired during a performance, is the fatigue more in your throat or in your diaphragm?

JOACIM: It's in my throat 99 per cent of the time.

BILL: Have you ever damaged your voice so much that you had to stop singing for a while?

JOACIM: Not by singing improperly. I have cancelled a couple of shows due to infections, but never from improper singing.

BILL: What do you do to keep your vocal stamina while touring?

JOACIM: The most important thing is to warm up before every single show, some days for ten minutes and some days for 30 minutes; it all depends on your daily vocal condition. Drink a lot of water before, during and after the show. Keep in mind that you shouldn't drink cold water – it should be room temperature at all times. As a vocalist you have to be the boring one and go to bed without partying every night, as alcohol really damages your voice. You should also stay away from too many cups of coffee.

While performing, you should listen to your body all the time. If you feel that your voice is getting a bit strained and tense, you should try to ease up a little bit. You don't have to take all the high notes every day. If you have six shows in a row, you have to keep that in mind and don't push too hard during the first one. Making a set list with regards to the vocalist is also something to keep in mind. Maybe you shouldn't start with the most difficult song for the singer. Pick a pretty easy song that helps you get into the mode, and that will open up your voice.

BILL: What do you do other than singing to keep your voice in shape?

JOACIM: Trying to get some exercise a couple of days per week. Drinking a lot of water even though I'm not doing a show. Trying not to scream too much while drinking alcohol. Avoiding too many cups of coffee. Trying to avoid dairy products, which put mucus on your cords. Sleeping as much as possible, that sort of thing.

BILL: What are the worst things a singer can do to damage his or her voice?

JOACIM: Smoke, take drugs, be in an environment where you have to yell in order to be heard, force your voice into a register that is not suitable for you. You should always write songs that fit the vocalist, not the other way around. A voice is something unique that you have to take care of.

BILL: What are the best ways for singers to improve their singing abilities?

JOACIM: There are no short-cuts to success. Practice is the only way to become a good vocalist if you're not a natural singer that was born with perfect pitch. If you want to become a singer, you should seek professional guidance from a vocal instructor, because it's impossible to hear yourself when you are doing things wrong.

BILL: Do you now, or have you ever, taken vocal lessons? If so, what areas did you focus on?

JOACIM: I took lessons for one year while going to the Musicians' Institute in Los Angeles. Apart from the basic vocal training, I tried to isolate my registers in order to gain some range in my falsetto. Another important thing is to work on your skills by ear, to listen to something and put it down on paper, learning to hear different intervals, to improve and learn the basics in music theory. At the present time, I don't take any lessons, even though I should. There's not really time for it. But my foundation was built during this period of time and I feel strong and secure enough to continue on my own.

BILL: Do you know if you're a tenor or a baritone?

JOACIM: I'm definitely a tenor.

BILL: What do you do to warm up for a performance?

JOACIM: I have some exercises that really work for me and that I have instructed others to try also, with great results. The first thing I do is to warm up my whole body with different stretching exercises. It could be anything from sit-ups to 'ugly faces'. Stretching the tongue is also important because of its involvement in vocal production. After my body is ready to sing, I start by doing vocal exercises with the easiest vowel sound that separates the cords: 'ay'. I start mid-register, going down really low, and then I climb up higher and higher, but as soon as I feel strain or tension I go back down again. I do this about three or four times, up and down.

The exercise goes like this: speak the word 'may' on pitch to sing. Start by singing the scale, on a comfortable note, from one to five. Then go down stepwise: 1-2-3-4-5-4-3-2-1. Then go down a half step at a time, doing the exercise on every step, until you feel that you can't go any lower. Now you should start climbing up the scales until you start feeling any kind of tension. Then it's important to stop and go back down again. The next time you reach the same 'problem' note, you'll feel that it's much easier. If you get bored with the 'may' sound you can change and sing 'mow'.

If you feel very tired in your voice before warming up, you can do a pre-exercise to get the voice ready. It goes like this: sing 'nah, nay, nee, noh noo' on the same note. Start at a comfortable note in the middle range and continue by descending chromatically a half step at a time. Try and get as low as possible and then ascend the scale until you're in your middle-upper range. Take it easy at first. Remember to think of 'sustained speech'.

When I'm done with both these exercises, I start to sing easy songs like lullabies or musical songs. These songs I know by heart and they are not that high in pitch. The benefit of knowing the song you are using as a warm-up is that you can focus 100 per cent on what you are doing, technically. These songs you can do in various keys. Never start too high. I always sing 'Close Every Door To Me' from *Joseph And The Amazing Technicolour Dreamcoat* when I warm up. It's a fantastic song that includes some cool intervals.

After this, I do the final exercise, where I return to the 1-2-3-4-5-4-3-2-1 exercise, but this time it's time for the head voice. Now the 'may' sound doesn't work and I replace it with 'oh'. I start on the same note I ended on the last 'may' exercise, ascending the scale chromatically until I feel any tension or strain, then I go back down. In this exercise, you feel pretty quickly when your voice is ready to do a show. Usually I do this two times.

While doing any of these exercises, it's important that you pre-jaw – open the jaw as in the beginning of a yawn – open the mouth and feel the cold spot in your mouth cavity while inhaling. Always remember to sing on the tail end of the breath.

BILL: Some people don't respect what metal singers do. In what ways is metal singing more or less difficult from other styles of singing?

JOACIM: In my opinion, metal singers need to control a wider singing range. Sometimes it's too high for our own good, though. All metal singers should use their strongest range more, their middle-middle or upper-middle, and use the upper range as a flavour to their singing.

Joe Comeau

Annihilator founder and guitarist Jeff Waters sums up Joe Comeau's voice when he says, 'Joe's best quality is sounding like whoever you want him to sound like... He has the ability to just clone any of the previous Annihilator singers, including myself, plus he has his own style.' Joe sang for '80s band Liege Lord and has played guitar for Overkill. His voice can do it all, as proven on *Carnival Diablos*, his first album as Annihilator vocalist.

BILL: Have you ever taken lessons?

JOE: Yeah. I recommend it to anyone who wants to further themselves and doesn't want to hurt their voice. I said, 'Hey, if I'm really going to do this, I want to make sure I'm doing it right.' I took lessons from the Hochstein School of Music, which is an affiliate of the Eastman School of Music here in Rochester, which is a killer music school. I had a female teacher who was trying to teach me Debbie Boone and I was like, 'Dude, I'm not into this.' She said, 'I know, but this is all we do here.' So I made sure I had the proper basics - how to use my voice correctly, how to warm up. That's the most important thing. When I got to the Debbie Boone shit, I bailed.

BILL: What do you do to warm up for a show?

JOE: Live, it's tough because, on our budget, we don't even have toilet paper, let alone a piano backstage. But it is important to warm up, and a lot of guys don't do it. What I try to do is I find someplace for me to go. Basically, over the years I've learned to warm up with scales by ear. If there's no place private for me to go, I'll sing or hum into a towel. That way, I'm not disturbing anybody. I start off low and work my way up, which is what you should do. You shouldn't be hitting the top of your range. You should be slowly warming it up over a period of 15 or 20 minutes.

With the hectic way it is on tour – you've got people nagging at you, pulling at you, there are interviews to do – I usually try to get some peace 30 minutes before the show, at least, just to get dressed and clear my head and warm up. When I was in Overkill playing guitar, I never took my guitar out and warmed up before a show, but vocally it's more important. Your body's the instrument. I bring a kettle with me. I get some hot water going a half-hour before the show. I don't drink coffee or tea; I just drink hot water. Then I'll keep that pot up on-stage. I try to get a road-crew guy to watch it for me, because it's important. It really helps loosen things up.

That's another important thing: you don't want to be out in the cold. If you have got to do a festival at 11 o'clock at night and it's, like, 45 degrees, you should stay warm somehow. You should have towels around your neck. You should be breathing into a towel so your voice stays warm. You should have hot liquid, preferably tea or water. Keep it warm, because breathing in that cold air can mess up your voice.

BILL: So on this upcoming tour, what are some of the things you're going to do to keep your voice in shape? I know that in Europe you've got to contend with a lot of smoke.

JOE: Yeah, which really sucks, because I don't even smoke. I've heard that a lot of my favourite singers smoke. I know Halford does. I was just on tour with him. I guess Brian Johnson does. I don't know how these guys do it. In Europe, I think the prerequisite for growing up is to have a cigarette in your mouth. And it's not a joke, man – it's unbelievable the way those people smoke. I'd say 90 per cent of people there smoke. The clubs are just insane, filled with smoke. The last tour was cool because me and Warrel, the singer from Nevermore – he doesn't smoke either – we made it a non-smoking bus. No one was allowed to smoke on the bus while we were travelling. It made a big difference.

BILL: Do you do any other things, like use a humidifier?

JOE: To tell you the truth, I love air conditioning. When we're in Europe you don't get it anyway. It's on in the bus, though. Even when we do have hotels, there isn't air conditioning in most of the hotels in Europe. They think we're strange with all this air conditioning. The clubs don't have air conditioning; the hotels don't have it - they sleep with the windows open and there's no screens, and the fucking bugs come in. Other than that, it's the strongest region for metal, so I'm not complaining.

For me, the most important thing on the road is to get a lot of sleep. I don't do drugs and I don't really drink much, but sleep is amazing. Sometimes I sleep 15 hours a day on the road. It's healing your body. If I'm taking a nap, I have to be up at least two hours before the show. Otherwise it's just like I got out of bed in the morning – there's no way I can sing.

BILL: You don't eat before a show either, do you?

JOE: I usually can't eat. Even when I was playing guitar, I'd eat a good three or four hours before I went on. When I was on tour with Halford, I noticed he did the same thing – he would eat after the show. You asked about this tour coming up: it's a little bit different because we're doing all festivals, so you got to think about 'Okay, today we're playing at four and it's 100 degrees. Tomorrow we're playing at 11 at night. We're more north, toward Sweden or something, and it's 45 degrees at night.' But at least you're outside in the fresh air and you don't have to worry about smoke and stuff.

BILL: Let's talk about technique a little bit. Have you ever tried to work on specific aspects of your voice, like your range or sustain?

JOE: The most important thing to remember is that your voice is a muscle. If you're singing correctly, you're gonna strengthen that muscle, so I find that the more consistently I sing – and I don't mean singing 12 hours one day, then having two days off; I mean like an hour or two a day for five days a week – after I do that for about two weeks I've got way more air, way more power, way more strength.

BILL: Would you say you're a tenor?

JOE: Yeah, my voice is more mid-range to tenor. I can go fairly deep, though. I have a pretty wide range, but it's more on the mid-range to higher end.

BILL: When you do the real high notes, is there a change in technique?

JOE: Basically, it's all pretty much the same - it's all singing with your diaphragm and keeping your airway open, letting the wind come through. A lot of guys sing incorrectly, tightening up and sing from their throat. A lot of people have heard that you've got to sing from your diaphragm. But what is your diaphragm? You've never seen it. You've only heard about it. You don't know what the hell it is.

If you're really interested in singing correctly, you need to take some lessons for a little while. High notes put a lot more demand on your vocal cords. You've got to stretch them thinner to reach those notes. But if you're singing correctly, it's just a matter of being warmed up. Then it's just a matter of singing like you always do, with a lot of wind from your stomach and chest. Just let it flow through.

BILL: Do you use any resonating sensations to guide you?

JOE: No. I'm pretty consistent. The thing is, I don't warm up enough. Usually, the first two or three songs, I'm saying to myself, 'Holy fuck! I'm never gonna make it through the show!' Everything is so closed up and I'm dying. Then there's a point where everything just opens up to where I'm warmed up and the shit just starts flying. I'm going to myself, 'I'm gonna fucking hit the next note higher!' That's how it works for me. Sometimes it's strange, you're getting ready to go on-stage and you're like, 'Man, what's wrong with me today? It feels like I got gobs of cheese in my mouth. Did I swallow milk or what?' Cheese and milk are bad things to have.

BILL: Too much phlegm.

JOE: Yeah. The most important thing is to be wet. I've found that drinking water throughout the day is good. By showtime, I'm all wetted up.

BILL: Do you have to piss every five minutes?

JOE: [laughs] Yeah! That's the good thing about being a singer: you can run off between songs or during a solo. Yeah, I'm not back there resting or taking a drink. I'm fucking pissing!

BILL: Anyway, you've got kind of a gravelly voice sometimes.

JOE: I like to sing like that. I can sing clean, but I don't feel like I'm doing my job. I don't know what it is. I feel like I'm not earning my money, like I've got to push more and I've got to kill myself... I could sing clean for months straight. *Carnival Diablos* is fairly clean. But there's a misconception that guys like Brian Johnson just get up there and scream – guys that sing clean, like Steve Perry, are just amazing singers. I mean, he's a great singer, but for almost anybody singing clean is easier than singing heavy. Brian Johnson is probably one of the hardest guys to sing like. I think heavy metal is the hardest music and the most physically demanding on all the band members. Pop or country is much easier than heavy metal.

BILL: Lots of people don't respect metal singers. They want to hear Ricky Martin. Do you ever go to karaoke and do mainstream stuff?

JOE: No, I never do, but when you're a singer in a band, people will meet you and say, 'Hey, give us a song.' I'm like, 'Get the fuck away from me,' you know? Relatives will do that, and people who aren't into the music business. They expect you to just sit there and start singing.

BILL: Like meeting a football player and asking him to block somebody.

JOE: Yeah.

BILL: I recently listened to the songs 'Time Bomb' and 'Shallow Grave'. Is there a technique you use to get that kind of gravel in your voice?

JOE: I've always been able to impersonate people very well. I always mimicked people when I was a little kid. I wanted to be Rich Little. I was really into that. And I have a really wide range, so I can sing thicker low stuff and higher stuff. I just basically took the songs Jeff [Waters, Annihilator guitarist] had written and tried to sing over them what I thought would fit. He was playing Shallow Grave for me, and this thing sounds just like freaking AC/DC. It's like really unbelievable. I hear Bon Scott all over this thing. So we talked about it, and it was like, 'Fuck it, man. If you can do Bon Scott, fucking do it.' It's real hard to say how it's done, though.

BILL: Okay, let me ask you this way. For instance, when you're doing that rough-sounding verse to 'Time Bomb', how loud are you singing? Are you wailing it?

JOE: Yeah, I sing pretty loud. In fact, we just got Shure wireless mics for this tour. The input gains have to be set all the way off. And the pad on the monitor board has to be pushed in, too. It's a button you push to reduce the level by 20 decibels. That's how loud I am.

BILL: So even the growly stuff on the verses is loud?

JOE: Yeah, it's all pretty loud. I think it's got to be a certain volume to get that attitude and power.

BILL: So, for you, a major part of being able to growl like that is high volume?

JOE: It has something to do with it. You can't do this stuff low. You'll have the same basic sound, but it's gonna sound like this dude trying to be mean and tough when he's actually singing like a fucking mouse. You don't have to rip your throat out, but you have to reach a certain level where you're singing with conviction.

I've found that the better vocalists do that because you don't want to use too much compression. You want a consistent volume. So I would see Halford go to scream and he would back the mic away a little bit. Mic technique is very important. If you move the mic too far away you lose the proximity effect and the low-end fullness to your voice. Then it sounds real thin, like you're singing into a horn.

BILL: Have you ever damaged your voice?

JOE: Yes. I did a Liege Lord reunion last year at the Wacken Festival in Germany. What happened was, after I left Liege Lord, I started a band with Sebastian Marino [Overkill] and Rob Mount [Ramrod], who is a killer drummer from right here in Rochester. This was before I was in Overkill and Annihilator. When it came time to do the Liege Lord reunion, the original guys bailed two weeks before the show, except for one original guy, Paul Nelson. So I recruited Sebastian, Rob and Carl Muscardini to play bass. We could only rehearse for four days, so I sang for eight hours a day. I hadn't sung these songs for three or four years. Then we flew for 27 hours to Germany with all these layovers and shit. Then we went on-stage at one o'clock in the morning, when it was really cold out. The response was great, but my voice was fucking hammered. It was a bit weird for two to three weeks after that. It just goes to show you that you can't just not sing for months and then sing for eight hours a day. You've got to work into it.

BILL: Anything you'd like to add?

JOE: Yeah. I want everyone to know to stick with what you believe in and really listen to yourself. Don't listen to anybody else. Anybody can become successful if they put their heart, mind and soul into it. In this style of music, it helps to be a nice guy, but you've got to know when to be aggressive, because you can easily get walked over.

BILL: By the record companies?

JOE: By anybody, you know? It's not an easy life. It's not an easy business to be in. People think that you're rock stars, travelling all around and buying all these fancy cars and houses and shit. Well, I'm still waiting for that myself. But I really love this music. This is really all that matters to me, and nothing's going to stop me from doing it. And anybody who has that attitude and works hard enough can be successful if they want to be. Even if you only have a little bit of talent, you can still be successful if you try.

Harry Conklin

Nicknamed 'the Tyrant', Harry has had extensive experience in singing opera and musical theatre but is known for his scorching lead vocals for metal stalwarts Jag Panzer.

BILL: Do you tend to sing loudly or at a conversational volume?

HARRY: I sing louder than conversation naturally. There is a feeling of control and a 'happy place' where my tone begins to resonate. Singing scales, practising parts or just plain fooling around are all in the same loud tone.

BILL: Do you sing as loudly in the studio as you do on-stage?

HARRY: Singing in the studio when your environment is in your head and effects – though ever so slight – are mixed for colour to reduce fatigue, I tend to not sing as loud but more controlled and in my body chamber. If you have been singing long enough, you can feel the difference of outward projection and inward compression. Compression is when you make the note small and contained, almost held back. Projection is when the note is going out and needs more air behind it to become full, rich and sustained.

BILL: Does your volume tend to increase as you go up the range?

HARRY: Volume decreases slightly and relaxation is maintained when the upper register is used. The fine line before full voice and head voice can be more evenly maintained when the body is relaxed and the mind is concentrating on the transition. Practising the full-to-head – falsetto – scales is important for achieving the right amount of push on the note when in head mode. When the transition scales are mastered – transition is undetected – then we can start pushing the head notes harder and harder until power, control, and relaxation is obtained.

BILL: Does your technique change as you go up the range?

HARRY: When singing in the upper register, one needs to concentrate on relaxing and controlling both body and throat. Using a bouncing vibrato in the throat helps relaxation and helps to control pitch. Sometimes the studio voice is compressed in such a way as to affect pitch control, or the guitars are distorted in such a way as to affect reference of pitch. Pitch can be the hardest thing to control when in the upper register due to the compressed tone in the studio. Yet, when singing live, one can relax and let go a little more, sitting in the tone.

BILL: On high notes, what sensations do you feel in your head?

HARRY: High notes should be lighter and relaxed compared to the growly lower notes. The feeling in my head is one of controlled breathing. Picture holding your breath for 30 seconds, then hold for another 30 seconds, letting out tiny breaths every four to five seconds. Then hold your breath for 40 seconds, letting out short breaths here and there. This is what one feels when singing in the high register. There is a slight light-headedness and, depending on the length of the sustained note, a little dizziness. This is normal and will subside with more practice and awareness.

BILL: Did you always have the range you have now or did you have to work at it?

HARRY: I had to work hard at achieving the 4.3-octave range I now have.

BILL: How does your technique differ when singing high notes clean from singing them with an edge?

HARRY: Technique differs greatly when applying the growly or evil, meaner tone. In the lower register, it is easier to bounce the larynx up and down for the mean tone, but up in the high range it is not healthy for this bouncing to be going on. But pushing from the abdomen means to stress and to strain for the high notes. The objective is to be as relaxed and unstressed as possible when in the upper range.

BILL: Is growling natural for you in all ranges?

HARRY: Growling is not a part of real and 'proper' singing. That is why opera people and pop singers don't like that sound. It is fun, however, to apply this experimental technique.

BILL: When singing, do you pay any special attention to breath support?

HARRY: When singing properly, there should always be strong breath support. Breathing is the life of the note. It is best to be cardio-vascularly fit in order to support long notes and hold them without fluctuation. There are fun ways to achieve proper breath support:

- Lay on your back with a phone book or slightly heavy object on your solar plexus – the upside-down V in your chest. Push the object with your solar plexus up and down – in and out – like push-ups, until the object will not rise any more.

- Fold an 8.5" x 14" sheet of paper in half lengthwise. Place it 16 inches away from your face in front of you on a table. Blow it over with one short yet powerful breath. Place the paper further and further away from your face until it will not fall over. This is your 'projection' goal.

- My favourite is the 'me-may-my-mo-moo' scale. Start by singing in one breath 'me-may-my-mo-moo' on one note. Then add an 'ah' or an 'oo' scale before the 'me-may-my-mo-moo' exercise. This can be very tiring and very good for you at the same time. Keep that breath *up*.

BILL: What do you to keep vocal stamina during touring?

HARRY: When I'm feeling not so hot or have a deeper voice in the morning than usual, it is a good sign that fatigue is setting in. Rest is the utmost important tool a singer of any style needs. Quality rest is hard to get when you're in a different place and climate every day or night.

Meditation can be the key to proper rest for the voice. You have to treat your body as an instrument and not toxify it and deprive it of good sleep. Talk only when you have to, in a low, unstressed tone. I've had days when I've stayed up late talking to fans and woke up not being able to speak. My bandmates become worried about my performance the next night yet will stay up all day in the tour bus keeping me from resting my instrument! I sing short, low scales before a show when I'm feeling rough in the throat. The occurrence of soreness has depleted through the years as I have grown stronger and more aware of what needs to be done for my voice.

BILL: Have you ever taken vocal lessons? If so, which particular areas did you focus on?

HARRY: I have taken, in total, seven years of vocal training, no less than three months at a time. The last time I contacted a voice instructor was three years ago. I feel that, if you want to know your instrument well, you must learn from someone who uses it all the time or who is trained the most in the profession.

BILL: Do you know if you're a tenor or a baritone?

HARRY: I am in the tenor-alto range. Some soprano – high B – can also be reached, yet not comfortably and consistently.

BILL: What do you do to warm up for a performance?

HARRY: My warm-up period before a performance has grown shorter as the years have progressed. I used to scale no earlier than one hour before a performance. Now I sing in the hotel room during dry rehearsal, and no more before the performance. Short humming scales and low talking is all.

Bruce Dickinson

Bruce is widely regarded as being one of the best rock singers in the world. Over the course of his 20-plus-year career, he has released nine studio albums with Iron Maiden and five solo albums, along with several live albums, selling over 50 million albums worldwide. Bruce has a full, rich voice with a wide range.

BILL: How did you start singing?

BRUCE: Well, musically speaking, I started off wanting to be a drummer, because I loved the fact that drums were really physical. I wanted to do something that used my body. Guitar and bass were almost too cerebral. I looked at guys like Ian Paice from Deep Purple and thought, 'Wow! He's an amazing drummer.' But also Keith Moon, who was wild and crazy. I thought, 'I'd like to play the drums like Ian Paice but be as wild and crazy as Keith Moon.' At the same time, I was using my voice a lot, mainly doing amateur theatre stuff. So I was using my voice, but mainly to perform in a different way. The two things kind of grew together when I realised that I was probably going to be a lousy actor because I couldn't take life seriously enough. All these people who were into acting, they took things so desperately seriously. I mean, I spend my days doing practical jokes. I thought, 'I can't be pretentious enough to be an actor.'

At the same time I was in a part-time band at school playing the bongos. We didn't have a drum kit, so I found some bongos and hit them really hard in this kind of mongoloid fashion. We only knew about two songs and one of them was 'Let it Be'. The guy who was the singer in the band was also the bass player, and he had a bass voice so he was totally unsuitable to sing the high bits in 'Let it Be'. It all sounded very stilted, so they asked me to shut up on the bongos. I thought I could hit some of the high notes, so I started singing and they said, 'Put the drums away. You're the singer now.'

At that time, I was into singers like Ian Gillan, Ian Anderson and a guy named Peter Hammill, who was in a band called Van Der Graaf Generator. He had this curious opera-with-razor-blades voice. He did weird sweeping things with his voice, and he used to tell these obscure, lengthy stories with his lyrics. At the same time, I really loved the energy in [Deep] Purple. So I came up with this fantasy world where you could do both things together: you could have these really dramatic, big, scary vocals that were telling complex stories. And that was my little dream that I had in the back of my head up until joining Maiden. To a lesser extent, I tried it in all the bands I was in.

BILL: Did you take any vocal lessons?

BRUCE: No. I'm basically self-taught. I joined a band in high school and did some gigs, then I went to university and joined a different band. One of the guys in that band was a guitar teacher, so I started learning guitar with the idea that I could then start writing songs.

Around this time, I had a girlfriend who went to a high-faluting girls' school. Everybody there got vocal lessons, and she'd written some of these things down in a book. She listened to me sing and said, 'You know, you've got quite a good voice, but you're much too stiff and tense.' I didn't want to admit it at the time, but I thought, 'That makes sense,' so I started reading. I had no idea about singing from the diaphragm or any of that stuff.

BILL: Were you losing your voice or experiencing any problems at the time?

BRUCE: I wasn't singing often enough for it to be a problem, but I just assumed that every time you sang, you lost your voice, and that was just the way it was supposed to be. So I started reading her notes. Then I went off and started doing some research. I went to all the public libraries, looked in all the encyclopedias. There was a very good book called *How To Sing*, which I've never seen again after I lost my copy of it. So I started taking all this information in. Then I started looking at all my favourite singers, taking their voices apart, like a mechanic would look at a car engine. I started analysing their voices, going, 'Ah, so he does *this* with his voice, and this other guy does *that*.'

Then I started looking at my voice, saying, 'What does my voice do? Which bits of my voice are its strengths? Which bits are its weaknesses?' I was particularly interested in tonality, the way that people make their voices fatter, richer and thicker. As soon as I hit on this idea of resonance – shifting your voice around the resonant cavities of your body – I got really excited. I thought, 'Wow, this is really cool. I see now. You can do lots of interesting things with your voice.'

So I spent a while just developing technique, like singing from my diaphragm, which sounded kind of stupid at first. Eventually, I got a feel for it. That's all it is – just a feeling. It takes a while of consciously using that muscle before you can use it unconsciously, and during that time your voice goes to hell because you're concentrating so much on trying to locate this diaphragm that your brain forgets about the song. But eventually it all comes together.

BILL: It's a retraining process. Let's talk about resonance. Do you have certain resonating sensations that help you gauge how well you're singing?

BRUCE: Well, when I'm warming up before a show – which I must confess I'm very lazy about – I try to do it as quickly and as painlessly as possible. I'm not some guy who locks himself away for 45 minutes. I figure that your voice is like a car engine, it only has so many miles in it, so I don't see any reason for wearing it out unnecessarily.

BILL: Especially if you're singing a lot already. You don't need to warm up as much then.

BRUCE: Yes. Precisely. You need to warm up a little bit, though, because you can really easily wreck your voice in the first minute of going on-stage.

BILL: So what do you do to warm up?

BRUCE: What I look for, first of all, is getting my diaphragm working, so I try to combine getting my diaphragm working with moving my voice around all its various resonant spaces. You basically have three voices – at least I do, anyway. I have a chest voice, a throat voice and a head voice. The head voice uses all the bone spaces and sinuses. It has a very nasal quality to it.

BILL: And you can feel it in your head?

BRUCE: Absolutely. You can feel it in your teeth. When I'm warming up, I like to produce my head voice with my mouth closed and my teeth together. I've got this sort of manic grin on my face and I try to shake my teeth loose – the front teeth – until the whole front of my face is vibrating. When I can do that fairly effortlessly, I join up the other two spaces. I will take a note – not singing loudly necessarily – and just hold it and vibrate, internally, this little space in my head. I'll move it around so the front of my nose, the back of my nose, my teeth and everything are humming like tuning forks. I try to keep that note as long as I possibly, possibly, *possibly* can without any tension in my throat muscles. So I'm trying to produce this column of air from my diaphragm that is energising all these sinuses.

BILL: And are you moving it up and down the range?

BRUCE: Well, I'm trying to keep it there for now. Then I might move it down and put my hand on my chest.

BILL: You mean you start out in the head voice?

BRUCE: Not necessarily. I generally start out in the chest voice because it's easier. Then I move straight to the head. I leave the throat part of it absolutely to the last, because the throat part is the bit that does all the damage. You can think of the throat voice as a choke. A lot of the tone for the rock voice comes from the throat. And it's really important to have your head and chest voice ready, because the chest voice is the anchor. It's the root.

BILL: It adds depth.

BRUCE: Yes. It gives the timbre and the tone and the depth. It's the rock that everything is built on. The head voice is what is going to cut through. It's what is going to carry that note straight into the sound spectrum where it needs to go. That's why so many singers with only about three notes in their range have been successful in rock bands – they can sing through their nose real good for about three notes. It just happens to cut through like a banshee. And they're good for a couple of albums, then everybody gets bored with their voice because they can't do anything else with it. Unfortunately, the volume at which rock bands play necessitates something very clear and simple to be sent through the microphone in order for the voice to carry over the music. Somebody who has a high-to-mid-range voice can do that. If you're a singer who wants to move outside of that, then you need a lot more firepower to get the flexibility over the sound of the band. It's difficult because it's a very hostile environment.

Rock bands are very hostile to singers. They're not built around singers. They're very loud, very primitive and very uncompromising and attacking in terms of their rhythms. It's not a nice environment to sing beautiful vocal shapes over. When you get a band like Maiden that wants to rigidly tie words to musical riffs, it's a very unhealthy singing environment. It forces you to do horrible glottal words and big octave jumps. I mean, Italian is not the language of opera for nothing – it's a very smooth language for singing in. Of course, if you restrict yourself to only words that work well singing-wise, you start restricting yourself in terms of lyrics, meaning and stories, so there's a constant battle, a constant compromise between the phrasing and the music.

BILL: I see. You want to tell the story as it's meant to be told, but you don't want to sing too many consonants on the high parts.

BRUCE: Absolutely. And Maiden is traditionally a nightmare for that, particularly when lyrics get written by non-singers. They tend to mumble them, thinking, 'Oh, that'll work.' Then they give it to the singer and say, 'Now you sing it an octave higher with some real power.' And I'm like, 'Well, you didn't sing it that way when you wrote it.' However, that is one of the things you get paid to do as a professional singer. It just comes with the territory. And, of course, it's one of the reasons you have technique. In fact, the only reason technique exists is to enable you to tell the story and express yourself through your voice.

Technique on its own is a crock of shit. It's absolutely useless. It's like guitarists who come along who can do huge pyrotechnic displays down the fingerboard but it leaves you feeling absolutely cold. It's all very impressive, but emotionally it's garbage. As far as singing goes, you can listen to guys who have amazing character to their voice but have very little technique at all – but by God, they can move you. In rock music in particular, if you chose to go down the road of singing in this big, dramatic, semi-operatic style, you've got to have some technique. Otherwise, you will lose your voice. You will not be able to get through it night after night.

BILL: In your voice, you have a very full, thick tone in your mid to high range, similar to an opera singer.

BRUCE: Yes. That happened in a very strange way. I was working with a producer called Tony Platt, who had been working with Mutt Lange on the *Back In Black* album as an engineer. I was in a band called Samson. We'd done an album already, in which I did my best Ian Gillan impression. My voice was quite thin back then – I could scream like a banshee – but it was all just barely under control. I got these ideas of technique in my head and I felt fairly safe and secure in my voice up to a certain point, where it would change over into falsetto. Then I'd let fly a big old scream. And I thought, 'Okay, great. That's me, then.'

But what Tony did was he made me sing what felt like completely out of my natural range. I'd get to the falsetto point and he'd say, 'Okay, now go do the whole song a fifth higher.' Then I'd get to the crucial top note and go, 'Well, I've got to go falsetto here because it sounds lame.' He'd say, 'No, don't do that. Just really belt it out in your natural voice.' So I did. Every two days I'd go to the studio and sing the vocal, then lose my voice. At the end of it all, I had this singer coming back out at me from the speakers who I didn't recognise as me. I was like, 'Who is this guy? That's not me.' I hated it.

BILL: But it was your real voice.

BRUCE: Yeah. Actually, it *was* me. It was the first time I'd ever heard me. Everybody else loved the way it sounded.

BILL: So it was a bit of a difficult transition, but it's just like strengthening any set of muscles to do something – there is always a period of awkwardness and strain.

BRUCE: Exactly. But then I tried to do it live and I lost my voice, and I was in despair. Then I suddenly remembered why I had learned all that stuff about technique, so I went back and learned how to produce this voice every night. In the studio, I had just made it by opening my mouth and screaming – I hadn't had time to think of a technique for producing it – so I sat down and figured it out.

BILL: And what did you discover?

BRUCE: It's about relaxing the throat at the crucial moment when your throat would tighten up and you say, 'I can't go any higher. I've got to go falsetto.' It's almost like loosening the gag reflex. You don't clam up at the crucial moment. At that moment, you have to really consciously allow the power of your diaphragm to take the air right through into your nasal passages. It's like you can almost bypass the throat entirely. You have to completely relax it. Up to that point, you can squeeze your throat to make your voice sound gruff or snarly, but once you get into the really, really high registers, you have to actively relax your throat to let these high notes come out.

There are muscles that hold the throat open. You can get a good couple of hours out of your voice that way. At that point, certainly in my case, I like to close it down. In my experience, you have a window of opportunity when you can produce this voice. It really is a question of when you're warmed up and ready to go. If you are, then go and do not stop. If you go for an hour and then you stop, then you try to go for another hour after you've had a tea break or whatever, you are setting yourself up to hurt your voice.

BILL: Have you ever really damaged your voice?

BRUCE: Oh, yeah. Fortunately, not permanently. Probably on half a dozen occasions I've had vocal strain from overuse of my voice, which has had me worried for a bit.

BILL: How long did it last?

BRUCE: The worst one was probably a week.

BILL: It's scary, though, when it's what you do for a living.

BRUCE: It's dreadful. It feels like a long time. I wanted it back the next day! The key thing to remember is you cannot re-string a voice. You have one shot. If you fuck your voice and develop nodes... Although they can remove the nodes, I've never heard a singer who had nodes who has been the same afterwards. I've been very lucky because I've never had any nodes or anything of that nature. The crucial thing is, if your voice is sick, don't be a hero. Get a good doctor, one who's not scared of your manager, one that will be willing to say, 'You must not sing for at least ten days,' or however long it is. And don't say, 'Oh, he said ten days. That means seven days.' Ten days means ten days. Take the doc's advice. One of the reasons I stopped, at a very early stage of my career, getting into this insane 'I can scream higher than you' thing is because I realised that your career is gonna last five minutes. There's always gonna be another gunslinger down the block who can scream like a banshee, and if you base your career on being able to scream like a banshee, the minute you can't do it, people say, 'He can't sing any more.' And you can't do it forever. There are a few exceptions to that, one notable being Rob Halford. He's a friend of mine and I have the greatest respect for him, but the man is a freak of nature in terms of his voice. I can't do what he does and I don't know how he produces that voice.

BILL: You mean the raspy, screaming part of his voice?

BRUCE: Yes. And it is not produced just in the studio. That is loud as hell in the room, acoustically. And he has a unique voice – it's an interesting voice – but I have no idea how he produces that. I've seen him, in the studio, be so hoarse that he can hardly talk, and he can go on and somehow this bestial thing comes out of him. It's amazing. I can't do it. But we are different singers, he and I. We have a different approach.

But in general, I looked at singers and thought, 'Well, it appears that, if you base your career on this, first of all you limit yourself artistically and secondly you are shortening your life span as a singer to no real advantage. So I made a choice that range and tone together were more important than what I described as parlour tricks. Most of the great singers have been able to go on to middle age. Look at Robert Plant, for example – he's still a terrific singer and he doesn't do the mad screams that he used to do. One of the most amazing singers that I ever saw was Tony Bennett. Jesus Christ, that man has an amazing voice. I still sing pretty high sometimes, but sometimes it's deceptive. Some people sing high and you say, 'That doesn't sound very high,' but when you try singing it, it's like, 'Wow!' One of those guys is Freddie Mercury. He's an incredibly difficult singer to cover, but it doesn't sound like that because it's effortless. You won't see many people trying to cover a bunch of Freddie Mercury songs, because not very many singers can deal with it.

BILL: Suppose you haven't sung for a while. How do you build your voice back up to strength without overdoing it too soon?

BRUCE: Well, let's say I haven't sung in six months, then we start rehearsing and building up to a show. I go in the first day and sing four or five songs. As soon as I start getting any kind of tension in my voice, I stop. The first thing that gets tired, usually, is my diaphragm. So, unconsciously you start tensing up. I think, 'Okay, diaphragm's tired,' and I go home. Then, the next day, I sing seven or eight songs. Then the third day I sing almost the whole set. Then I'll have a day off. Then I'll come back the next day and sing the whole set. Once I've gone through the whole set, I start piling on the pressure. My diaphragm's up to speed, so I really start giving it some stink, trying to get some extra power and volume. Then, of course, the voice will get tired again, for different reasons now – now it's the throat muscles that are working, so it takes another week blast through that barrier. By the time we get to the first gig, it'll be survivable and it'll sound good, but the first show after the first day off, that's when it really starts to sound a lot better. For the first week or two of the tour, you're still making your voice stronger. Then, although there are ups and downs from day to day, you can generally count on everything being okay.

BILL: Are there any special techniques you use keep your voice in shape?

BRUCE: Well, one bit of good advice I got from a throat doc was to cut out dairy products.

BILL: Because they produce mucus and phlegm?

BRUCE: Absolutely, and phlegm is a horrible subject. There was some German opera singer in the late 19th century who wrote a whole book about phlegm, which I think is going a bit far, but it is a number-one enemy, so avoiding dairy products is a real good start. I tend to avoid eating for at least a couple of hours before a show. In general, I avoid eating big meals at all times. You just want to keep your tummy nice and comfortable all the time so your diaphragm has lots of space, so I tend to graze throughout the day. I have a flask of black coffee that I take on-stage with me and I have a bottle of water. That's it.

BILL: Why coffee? Any special reason?

BRUCE: It's just something warm to drink and it keeps me awake. I used to have a little facial sauna that people use for getting their zits out. I used to have one bubbling away all the time on the side of the stage so, if there's a lot smoke or dust in the air, I can just run off and breathe some steam for a couple of minutes. But in recent years, I've found that I haven't really needed that. Off-stage, the main thing is plenty of sleep. If your body is tired, your voice will be tired. Say on a day off you go and play a couple of hours of soccer. It's surprising how much that will take out of your voice the next day. So, since I run around on-stage a lot, I'm fit enough as it is. On days off, I tend to be as lazy as hell on the road. I hang around, lay in bed, watch TV. Some days I'll just be in my room all day. It works wonders. On the day of the show, if you just sack out and loll around all day, then go out for a quiet walk or something, then come back and lie down for a couple of hours it's amazing how much that will do for your performance.

BILL: What about air conditioning? Is that a problem?

BRUCE: I hate air conditioning. Air conditioning is the bane of my life. When I'm not singing, I really don't give a shit. I'm like, 'Turn it up to the max and let's dehydrate everything in sight!' The worst thing for me was when we were travelling a lot on buses. I was just in a terrible state when I'd get off an overnight trip on a bus. There was no humidifier in the world that would fix what they did to you on buses. You'd come out feeling like a prune, all moisture gone.

With a lot of venues now, you really have no choice, unfortunately. They've got what I call fascist air conditioning: it's mandatory that it be on. I sweat an awful lot when I'm on-stage, so when you're wet, you suddenly discover all these drafts. You're standing on-stage and there's a gale blowing across the stage. There's a pressure difference between one side of the hall and the other side, and the air conditioning is just going *whoosh!* It's really distracting. My favourite venues are old general-admission cowsheds with tin sides and no air conditioning at all. I'll put up with the 90-degree heat. What I can't deal with are these frigid Vegas-style places. It feels completely wrong to be running around for an hour and a half then come off dry as a bone.

BILL: Let's talk about high notes. You sing pretty much in full voice. You don't use falsetto very much.

BRUCE: No. What happened was, as soon as I started pushing my voice into these upper registers, the difference between my falsetto voice and my full voice became almost nil.

BILL: So is there any difference in your technique when you sing the high notes as opposed to the chest and middle notes?

BRUCE: There is much more tension in the abdomen because you've really got to get that column of air flying up. You've really got to get some power out of your abdomen. It's like you're trying to squeeze a plum through the back of your nose. That's what it feels like when you're doing one of these high notes – you're trying to squeeze this plum that's buried somewhere in the middle of our head. You're trying to squeeze it out through the top of your nose. At the same time, it almost feels like there's a string that goes from your sacrum right through your body and out the top of your head. It's like the sound is being pulled out of the top of your head. That's the feeling. It involves the whole body.

BILL: Have you ever felt light-headed after singing high notes?

BRUCE: Oh, God, yes. Absolutely. In the studio, I get the most fearful headaches when I'm singing full on. I feel dazed.

BILL: In heavy rock, there is good use for edgy or raspy singing. Although you sing mostly clean, what do you do to get that occasional edgy sound?

BRUCE: Well, singing fairly clean is a result of trying to keep the throat open. I can put a little bit of raspiness in it just by relaxing the muscles that are keeping the throat open. It's a bit like a guitarist who has a wah-wah pedal – you only have to touch the pedal a tiny, tiny bit to produce the effect. In singing, that's the way you limit the damage.

One thing I've always had is a fairly loud natural voice. Sometimes it can be a problem. From doing unplugged shows, singing with no microphone in a room with a couple of acoustic guitars and a bunch of people, I've made an interesting observation about where I'm projecting my voice. I'm projecting my voice about six to ten feet ahead of me. I'm trying to fill the room. Now, if I do that for a couple of weeks and then I go into a rehearsal room with a microphone and monitors, I'll have a terrible time. I've been used to filling the room with sound whereas now I only have to project my voice about an inch in front of my mouth. It's not a good thing to mix the two types of singing. You can do an awful amount of damage to your voice by unexpectedly saying, 'Let's go do an unplugged thing' in the middle of touring with monitors and a microphone. You'll expect to get a certain sound, and when you don't get it, you tend to push too hard.

BILL: In the studio or live, are there any effects that you favour over others?

BRUCE: I don't use any effects. I mean, they use effects on my voice out front, but when I'm monitoring in the studio I have no effects in my headphones. I dislike anything other than a natural voice. And I have it EQ'd absolutely flat.

BILL: You want the natural sound.

BRUCE: Yes, completely, because without the natural sound I don't have any information. Any time a piece of electronics comes between my voice and my ears, I don't know what I'm singing. I get confusing feedback because my body is telling me I'm singing one thing and this noise coming back in my headphones is telling me I'm singing something else. I don't like that; it's too weird. I don't like reverb or anything. Lots of effects can make you feel good, but when you strip it down and listen to the raw data, it might not sound so good. But if you start with an amazing performance, you probably don't need to add that much at all, just a bit of natural room sound or a little delay. I don't tend to have a lot of stuff on my voice −principally delays to thicken things up a little bit. In fact, most times in the studio I don't even double-track the vocals. You're hearing just a single voice. I find that, if I double-track it, it doesn't sound as powerful. What everybody likes in Maiden is for everything to sound spiky and identifiable.

BILL: Let's touch a little bit on equipment and vocal effects. In terms of equipment, do you have any favourites?

BRUCE: For a long time I resisted radio mics. The early radio mics were fantastic if you didn't have much of a voice because they incorporated a big compressor. If you had no voice, the compressor would boost the signal and you'd have a great sound. If you had a loud acoustic voice, the mic would diminish it. So you would get frustrated that, when you belted out a high note, it didn't sound like it was being belted out when it came back through the monitors. So you'd over-sing and all of a sudden...bing! You'd lose your voice. So I went back to table mics, and the difference is astounding.

BILL: What do you use live?

BRUCE: I was always using just a straight Shure SM58. We did try out the beta 58s and I actually ended up going back to the regular 58s. But we also found that there was a big variation in some of the capsules because they started making the capsules in Mexico after a while. If you can find some old 58s with the old capsule, they really sound amazing. Shure was always trying to get me to use a radio system, and they came up with a system that really worked. I used it at first only in certain areas of the stage where I knew the vocal levels were going to be good and the band level was going to be relatively low. Then they came up with the SM57 version of the radio mic. That's what I use now. I was quite surprised that, out of using an SM57 and their radio system, I'm really close to what I used to have with an old 58 and a cable. So, for ease of set-up, I now use a radio system all the time.

BILL: How about in the studio?

BRUCE: In the studio it tends to be a regular Neumann U87. But I've used all kinds of things. *Number Of The Beast* was recorded on a Shure SM7, which is a dynamic mic usually used for bass drums, and on *Somewhere In Time*, we used a mic that is normally used for recording trombones. So I've used many different kinds of mic, which helps keep things interesting.

David Draiman

David Draiman's voice is the quintessential nu-metal voice: maximum power, growl and attitude without the loss of melody. Disturbed's platinum debut album, *Down With The Sickness*, rocketed to number 26 on the *Billboard* album charts. They've co-headlined Ozzfest and have taken the world by storm on their own headlining tour.

BILL: David, have you ever had any vocal lessons?

DAVID: Yes, I have. A year's worth, actually.

BILL: What did you work on in those lessons?

DAVID: There are several things that, as a rock singer, you need to work on, depending on how aggressively you go, vocally. The key issue is always where you are singing from. The habit of many rock singers, unfortunately − especially in this new genre of metal − is that they sing from the throat, which is really the worst possible thing that you can do.

BILL: You mean you've got to sing from the diaphragm, right?

DAVID: Well, not really. Anybody that tells you 'Sing from your diaphragm' is lying to you because the diaphragm is not a muscle that is under your conscious control. It's an unconscious muscle; it's not meant to be used consciously. And, in fact, you can go ahead and do a little experiment with me if you want to, to see if I know what the fuck I'm talking about. Go ahead and stand up.

BILL: Okay [stands up].

DAVID: Okay, squeeze your diaphragm. Squeeze where you believe your diaphragm is, which would be right underneath your rib cage. Just consciously try to squeeze it.

BILL: [squeezes abdomen] You can't squeeze it.

DAVID: What happens to your body when you try?

BILL: You're actually squeezing your abdominal muscles.

DAVID: Right, and also your throat closes up, doesn't it?

BILL: Yes, it does!

DAVID: Right. And if your throat is closed, it's kind of difficult to get air and sound through it. That is the principal mistake that most people make when they try to figure out where their power is supposed to come from when singing this type of music. You have muscles that help with your breathing that are around your lower to middle back. Those are the muscles that should be used for advanced technique and additional power in this type of singing. Your ribs should expand, giving your lungs more capacity, and your diaphragm should be completely relaxed. The muscles that you're using are your breathing muscles in your low to mid back.

BILL: Yet the diaphragm does flex as you inhale.

DAVID: It does, but not consciously. That's the whole thing. You're not supposed to think about your diaphragm. The minute you start thinking about it and worrying whether or not it's being flexed, that's when the rest of your body begins to tense. Your diaphragm is going to work perfectly. That's the way it was created. You don't have to consciously think about your diaphragm. What you have to be is 100 per cent relaxed so that there is as little tension in your body as possible, because tension absorbs sound.

Everybody always tries to teach singers about resonance. They say, 'You need to resonate. The sound needs to resonate throughout your body, through the back of your head, in different areas.' These are focal points that they try to point out to you. And sound cannot resonate through something that is stiff. You need to be relaxed. The most important part of any warm-up a singer does prior to singing is actually relaxing themselves, making sure that all the parts of their body are loose.

BILL: I agree. It's important to loosen up physically and mentally. What else do you do to warm up?

DAVID: I vocalise. I'll go through scales and, depending on where I happen to have a little bit of difficulty on the scale, that is the area that I concentrate on.

BILL: Let's talk about touring. When you're on the road, what do you do to keep your voice in shape? I'm sure doing interviews doesn't help!

DAVID: It doesn't affect me drastically, but speaking in general is a lot more difficult on the voice that singing.

BILL: Do you use a humidifier in your room?

DAVID: Occasionally I'll use a humidifier, but too much humidity is no good, either. In the beginning, I used to bring the humidifier and just flood the room with humidity. Then you have a good chance of aspirating a little bit of the moisture in the air, and then you end up with an irritation, which can lead to an infection in the lungs. And the humidifier needs to be cleaned constantly because it can spew forth airborne bacteria. It's not a simple thing. It is always important to keep yourself hydrated, and humidity in the environment will certainly help you to do that, but it is not a be-all end-all, by any means. I think that singers in general are at the greatest risk of damaging their instrument because your body is your instrument. It's not like being a guitar player; it's not like being a drummer, where if you're a little bit ill or something you can still play. When your body is not happy, it will affect your tone, your resonance, everything.

BILL: Can you speak a little bit about technique in the high range as it pertains to hitting the head voice?

DAVID: Again, the most important part is to make sure you remember that, when you're trying to hit a high note, posture is an issue. If you have your body in a tensed or clenched-up position, it's going to be that much more difficult and damaging to attempt to hit the higher note.

BILL: How about growling technique?

DAVID: It's hard to describe. The issue is making sure that your throat is not being utilised completely. You're gonna need to use it in some way to generate that type of sound, but you should remember that it's always going to have to remain open, primarily. People who try to attain a gravelly voice by closing up the throat and trying to force air through it are going to end up hurting themselves. There are plenty of singers who do that and develop nodes and callouses that effect their voices for the rest of their lives.

BILL: Do you tend sing at a loud volume?

DAVID: I typically sing very loud, but the level of the volume of my voice does tend to fluctuate. Then again, that really is dependent on the song more than anything else.

BILL: Do you tend to get louder in the high range?

DAVID: Ideally, you shouldn't have to get louder, but sometimes when you're stretching it takes a little bit more effort to go through the entire duration of the stretch.

BILL: Do you know if you're a tenor or a baritone?

DAVID: I've been told that I'm a tenor, but I don't know if that's 100 per cent accurate. I have a pretty wide range.

BILL: Who has influenced you as a singer?

DAVID: Growing up, I listened to punk rock and new age. I wasn't traditionally a metal guy. The only metal bands that I really embraced in the '80s were bands like Metallica, Maiden, Priest, Pantera and bands like that. I wasn't really a big glam-metal guy – never my thing. In terms of influences, currently I'd have to say that Maynard James Keenan from Tool is a tremendous influence – more like an inspiration, really. I try to base my own style on what the song brings out of me at that particular point in time, not really looking toward anyone else for a stylistic influence *per se*.

Rik Emmett

Rik is one of Canada's most respected musicians, an award-winning guitarist, singer, songwriter and producer with his own independent label. As a founding member of Triumph, his blazing guitar solos and vocals helped push the Toronto-based trio into multiple gold and platinum sales worldwide in the '70s and '80s and earned him a spot in the Canadian Rock

Hall of Fame. Triumph had several worldwide hit singles, including 'Lay It On The Line', 'A World Of Fantasy', 'Hold On' and 'Fight The Good Fight'.

BILL: How young were you when you started singing, how did you get started and who influenced you?

RIK: I started as a first soprano in the church and school choirs when I was around eight or nine years old. My mom was also a choir member, and she loved to sing around the house. Around 1964, The Beatles became heroic, especially McCartney. As I grew older, my influences became more eclectic: Paul Simon, James Taylor, Ian Gillan of Deep Purple, Jon Anderson of Yes, Robert Plant of Led Zeppelin.

BILL: Do you tend to sing loudly or at a conversational volume?

RIK: Either way. Dynamics is a part of musical expression. If you can only sing loudly or softly, you're missing out on a fair bit of expressive range, wouldn't you say?

BILL: Does your volume tend to increase on high notes?

RIK: Not necessarily. It depends on what the music calls for. A soft falsetto can be very appropriate, and of course the piercing falsetto wailing of Ian Gillan on something like 'Child In Time' or Robert Plant on 'Immigrant Song' is also pretty effective stuff.

BILL: Does your technique change as you go up the range?

RIK: Yes. Head tones are often created by a tighter throat.

BILL: On high notes, what sensations do you feel in your head?

RIK: I don't think about 'head sensations'; I think about listening to the pitch and tone. I think about where the melody sits against the harmonic content. I think about breath control. I try to get my mouth wide open and get the notes to drive from the top-back of my throat. It's a common trick that singing with a 'smile' helps pitch that's in danger of going flat.

A common problem that I often hear is singers over-singing, pushing their voices too hard, and they go terribly out of pitch simply because they can't hear themselves. When you get good pitch against the musical background, you can really feel the natural blending of your sound waves with the other harmony. If you're out of tune, it will feel distinctly uncomfortable − sound waves beating against each other in irregular patterns and rhythms.

BILL: How do you manage the register change from chest to head voice?

RIK: A natural break occurs in almost every throat.

BILL: Did you always have the range you have now or did you have to work at it?

RIK: High-end range was always natural and easy, [more so than] a smooth and powerful bottom end. When my pipes get tired I have a problem with the upper middle of my range. I lose power and control there, around the chest/head break point.

BILL: How do you improvise when you're having a bad-singing day?

RIK: I don't. I stick to the prescribed melodies and I don't mess around. When in doubt, lay out − a good musician's creed.

BILL: What burns your voice out the most when singing?

RIK: Having to put edge on break-point notes − for me, from about a G to a B. Mostly, I get burned out from having to do talking on show days or rehearsals right before a gig.

BILL: If you get tired during a performance, is the fatigue more in your throat or in your abdomen?

RIK: I sing with my whole body. I feel the effects of fatigue everywhere because it's all about oxygen in the bloodstream. As I get older, I actually get a little light-headed sometimes.

BILL: Have you ever damaged your voice?

RIK: Laryngitis. I shut up for a few days and my voice started coming back. There's no substitute for rest and hydration.

BILL: What do you do to keep your vocal stamina during touring?

RIK: Try not to talk. Try not to sit in direct air conditioning. Try to sip from bottled water constantly. Don't smoke. Don't drink. Get plenty of rest and proper sleep and proper diet. It ain't rocket science, kids.

BILL: What are the worst things a singer can do to his or her voice?

RIK: Go to a soccer, baseball, football or hockey game and scream blue murder for a few hours. Or rehearse for six hours straight, singing full out.

BILL: What are the best ways for singers to improve their singing abilities?

RIK: Become better musicians. Have better time, better feel, better intonation, phrasing and note selection. Know themselves better, know their limitations and choose music that works to their particular strengths and avoids their weaknesses. Don't try to do too much. Do what comes naturally and work on developing the natural range of your interpretation.

BILL: Have you ever taken vocal lessons?

RIK: Except for choir practice as a kid? Nope.

BILL: How do you warm up for a performance?

RIK: I do a little vowel singing occasionally and rubberise the vocal cords over my range. I'm not huge on warm-ups or exercises; I like to sing songs. I generally make up melodies in either the Dorian or Aeolian mode and improvise little Celtic folk melodies using nonsense vowel sounds.

BILL: Raspy singing is common in rock music. How does your technique differ when singing high notes clean versus singing them with a raspy edge?

RIK: Throat rasp, yeah. It kills me, though. I'm not keen on it, and I'm not much good at it. It makes me sound like a Rod Stewart impersonator. It doesn't suit me. The older I get, the more I value clean notes. I've always been more of a clean singer. Rasp always sounded affected to me, pretentious, like I was trying too hard. It works for others, but it's not my cup of tea.

Andy Franck

Andy is lead singer for two stellar European metal acts: Brainstorm and Symphorce. His voice has a powerful, rich tone with good range.

ANDY: When I was 14 years old, I started to sing in a school band. Nobody wanted to sing and I wanted to play guitar, but this was the only chance for me to get in the band, so I bought myself a microphone. I grew up with bands like KISS, Judas Priest and Iron Maiden, so Rob Halford and Bruce Dickinson are my favourites. Sometimes I played bass or guitar, but I always turned to singing again.

Bands like Lightning, Panama, Outrage and my first solo band, Whisper, won't mean much to you, huh? But we recorded many demo tapes and played a lot of live shows. When I turned 21, I re-united Ivanhoe, who had previously broken up. We recorded three albums and played many shows around Europe. In 1998 I founded Symphorce, and I'm proud to say that finally I am doing the kind of music I always wanted to. Also, since October 1999, I've been a member of Germany's finest, Brainstorm.

BILL: Do you tend to sing loudly or at a conversational volume?

ANDY: My problem is that I have a very loud voice, so I have to sing loud, but I like to change my kind of singing a little bit.

BILL: Do you sing as loud in the studio as you do on-stage?

ANDY: Yes! It doesn't matter where you are – I want to kick ass. If there's a crowd, okay. If not, I'll kick the producer's ass!

BILL: Does your volume tend to increase as you go up the range?

ANDY: A little bit! Over the last few years, I learned how to deal with the microphone playing live.

BILL: Does your technique change as you go up the range?

ANDY: Hmm. My mouth always stays the same, but if I go up the range I use a bit more power. But this is very important, because if you can't do it that way, your voice will sound very thin.

BILL: What parts of your range give you the most trouble?

ANDY: It's funny, but sometimes more the lower notes. But I think there I do use that kind of power I use in higher ranges, so I really have to concentrate on the lower ones.

BILL: Did you always have the range you have now?

ANDY: Most of the range I had when I started, but now I concentrate on using the range at the right position. But as it sounds now, yes, I had to work on it. I always had my heroes, and I'm honest if I'm saying that I checked out their style.

BILL: How does your technique differ when singing clean when compared to singing with a growl?

ANDY: Hmm. It's still me, but you can use words in different ways.

BILL: Does your throat tighten up during growling? Is there more push from the abdomen?

ANDY: Yeah, a bit more, so you can give words more power and expression. It helps a lot and makes your lyrics more sensible. But my throat doesn't really tighten during growling. When I started singing, I was always a bit flat in the low range, but when I used a bit more power, I hit the note, and it's always very important for me. With all my latest releases, I'm satisfied for the first time with every note on both albums. On earlier releases, I was sometimes a bit angry that some notes were a bit wrong.

BILL: Is growling something natural for you in all ranges? Did it require much practice?

ANDY: No, my normal voice is very clean, but I grew up with all those thrash-metal bands in the '80s and I always wanted to have this growl feeling in my voice, so I practised and started listening to a lot of different singers. But still I always kept my normal, clean voice, so I can mix that if I want to, and it gives my kind of singing a very personal feeling.

BILL: When singing, do you pay any special attention to your breathing or any other physical sensations?

ANDY: When I was younger, I always made the same mistake: I went on, ran around and after the second song I was totally down, so I had to take a rest and stand there for more than three or four songs. Nowadays I go up and start acting but always not too much, so I can stand this for the whole show. Doesn't matter if we're playing 45 minutes or two hours. But breathing... I have a very strange kind of breathing while I'm singing because I played clarinet for more than 14 years and this is where I got my style from. Very strange.

BILL: How do you improvise when you're having a bad-singing day?

ANDY: I do not act too much. Most of the time I'm running around, but when

I feel 'Uargh, this won't be a good day for singing' I start concentrating on singing and not using my throat too much, so it can maybe be better the next day. Something else: let the people sing the lines. They think, 'Hey, cool, he lets us sing it,' and you can just relax and let them do the problem parts. I hate those days. For me, a long warm-up is the most important thing. I drink a lot of water and stop talking until three hours before the gig.

BILL: What burns your voice out the most when singing?

ANDY: Smoke. It's not only that I can't see anything any more; it's that it really makes your throat not wet enough. So if you have smoke or fog on-stage, you have to drink, drink and again drink. But no alcohol – that burns my voice just more. Normal water is for me still the best, but what I really hate when we're on-stage is smoke. Yes, that really burns my voice.

BILL: If you get tired during a performance, is the fatigue more in your throat or in your abdomen?

ANDY: I always try not to sing with the throat. When I get tired, it's more in my stomach or diaphragm. That's a critical point because at that time I start using my throat, and this is not good for the next day.

BILL: Have you ever damaged your voice so much that you had to stop singing for a while? If so, what happened?

ANDY: Not for a while, but for one show. It was nothing special, but when we were playing in Italy I had to do four radio and TV interviews in two hours, and in the background all the other bands had their soundcheck, so it was really loud inside and I had to scream. So when we went on-stage, I sounded like Phil of Pantera. But the fans were cool and sang most of the songs for me. They knew the lyrics. Good crowd.

BILL: What do you do to keep your vocal stamina during rigorous touring?

ANDY: I just drink a lot of water, and I do not talk too much right before or right after the show. But, for me, I believe that your vocal fitness depends on your physical fitness. You know, since I do a lot of jogging and so on, I never had any problems with my voice on tour.

BILL: What do you do, other than singing, to keep your voice in shape?

ANDY: As I said, I believe that the fitness of your voice really depends on the fitness of your whole body, so I do a lot of jogging and mountain biking.

Why? For myself, I found out that, if I'm not in good shape, after a few songs I start singing only with my throat, not with my diaphragm. So as long as I'm fit, I think my voice works much better.

BILL: What are the worst things a singer can do to damage his voice?

ANDY: Talk too much! We're singers, not storytellers. And do not whisper, because whispering really kills your voice.

BILL: What are the best ways for singers to improve their singing abilities?

ANDY: Start singing – and if the people don't leave the hall, maybe it's okay.

BILL: Do you now or have you ever taken vocal lessons?

ANDY: No, never. When I was about 14 I wanted to have lessons, but that was too expensive. It's practising, practising, practising. The best place to practise and warm up is in the bathroom after you've had a hot shower.

BILL: Do you practise regularly, or do you mostly just warm up and then hit the stage?

ANDY: I always do a 15-minute warm-up before I hit the stage. I never had a problem when I got on-stage without any warm-up, but it's not so good if you're on a tour because not warming up before the show kills your voice.

BILL: What do you practise on - scales, songs? Would you share one of your favourites for the book?

ANDY: No songs, but I also do not really practise scales because I've got this kind of a throat-and-diaphragm warm-up. When you see me warming up you will always hear a 'Brrrrrrrrrrrr' or a bad 'Uuuuaaaapppp' – no kidding! But this is what a guy from Brazil told me. I tried so many different versions, but this was the very best one! I love it, but it sounds strange.

BILL: Is that 'Brrrrrrrrrr' like a flapping of the lips or a rolling of the tongue?

ANDY: 'Brrrrrrrrrrrr' is like a rolling of the tongue. Like you say, 'Rrrrrrrrattlesnake', for example. It's not sustained notes. It always goes up and down, the whole range.

BILL: And 'Uuuuaaaapppp?'

ANDY: It goes down. It's all in the throat. It sounds like a siren a little bit. The other guys always look very strange at me. The whole thing is not done on the same pitch. Always up and down. For the first five or six minutes, my mouth is closed, like I'm humming, but when I'm getting warm I have to open it. And also it's very important to do it while you roll your head from one side to the other.

BILL: In what ways is metal singing more or less difficult than singing other styles?

ANDY: You know, I'm sure there are many metal singers out there that can't even sing one note – but of course there are many more pop singers out there that don't know what to do with a mic, so they use studio equipment as much as they can and their voices sound great. So metal singers are, I think, honest. And metal singers can bring down, on one CD, ten different persons with ten different feelings. This is something only a metal singer can give the fans.

Angela Gossow

Angela is the ferocious lead singer for Swedish metal band Arch Enemy. Her vocal style is characterised by deep growls and scorching screams.

BILL: How young were you when you started singing?

ANGELA: I started vocals in 1991. I was 17 back then. I also joined my first band, Asmodina, in 1991, which was a German death-metal band. In 1998, I founded my own death-metal band, Mistress. I left Mistress in 2000 when I got the gig in Arch Enemy.

BILL: Does your technique change as you go up the range?

ANGELA: I use mostly the resonance rooms in my head for the higher notes. Deeper notes are more vibrating in the chest. I don't really push any more than I would normally on high notes because this would hurt the vocal cords.

BILL: On high notes, what sensations do you feel in your head?

ANGELA: Vibration in the skull bones and tickling in my nose.

BILL: Have you ever worked on increasing your range?

ANGELA: I increased the upper range for clean vocals, but I had to work on it.

BILL: How do you warm up for a performance?

ANGELA: I start with a bit of stretching, then go on to humming and lip trills to make sure that I am singing without too much air. The voice shouldn't sound breathy. I do some easy melody patterns as well as some low and high screams.

BILL: What do you do to keep your voice strong while touring?

ANGELA: I do warm-up exercises and stretching every morning before I start to talk. I repeat the same procedure before the show. Some days I don't talk at all when my voice is weak. I go running and get massages to keep my muscles flexible. I usually have a humidifier in the hotel room and drink three to five litres of water every day.

BILL: What burns your voice out the most when singing?

ANGELA: People who smoke and long vocal passages without breathing gaps.

BILL: How do you improvise when you're having a bad-singing day?

ANGELA: I do a slow and long warm-up in the morning and before the show. I reduce the loudness of the vocals and, if necessary, don't talk at all before the show. Sometimes I use hot steam inhalations and have warm water to drink.

BILL: In your opinion, what are the best ways for a singer to improve his or her singing ability?

ANGELA: Have a good vocal coach who can judge you from an objective point of view. Do exercises daily.

BILL: What do you work on in your vocal lessons?

ANGELA: I focus on timing, articulation and breathing techniques. Breath control and support are important for growling.

BILL: So how does your technique differ when singing clean notes from singing them with an edge? Do you consciously have to tighten or push more to growl?

ANGELA: The vocal cords close when you sing clean. For growling, they are wide open while lots of air is pushed through. The gargling sound develops in the throat with the help of lots of throat constriction. It's not good to push more from the abdomen because muscular pressure means pressure on the vocal cords, and this can lead to nodules or bleeding cords sooner or later, which no singer needs! The breath has to be supported from the diaphragm, so you don't use more than necessary to create the growling sound.

Bruce Hall

Bruce is lead singer for Order Of The Illuminati – formerly known as Agent Steel – one of metal's veteran bands. Bruce has a strong, versatile voice.

BRUCE: I started singing when I was about 17. That's really late for most people. For some reason, it just really struck me. I mean, I practised incessantly – relentlessly – for at least three hours a day for most of my life, much to the chagrin of my family, my roommates and my neighbours... Most people are not like Chris Robinson [of The Black Crowes], waking up with this voice born into them. I think most people have to put a little effort into it. I had to put a lot of effort into it. I might be naturally musical, but I'm not naturally gifted for singing.

BILL: Did you have pitch problems?

BRUCE: My pitch in the beginning was really sharp. I used to sing higher than everything. I don't know if that was just an effort to be louder than the music that I was singing to or what. Certain singers that I idolise, like Dickinson, have a tendency to be a little bit sharp, too, so I was kind of following them. It wasn't until I started religiously singing Kansas songs that my pitch became more stable.

BILL: So who are your influences?

BRUCE: Dickinson, Klause Meine, Halford, Tate. Those guys are the main core. Steve Walsh probably had the most to do with why I consider myself to be a qualified singer. My roommates just hated listening to me sing. They'd say, 'You're killing yourself with all that Maiden stuff. It's not teaching you anything.' I was just beaten to death. As far as my voice goes, that was the best advice I ever took. Steve Walsh is the biggest influence on my voice, though you won't hear it. Stylistically, I'm just not that into it.

BILL: Do you still practise as much as before?

BRUCE: No. Maybe an hour a day, mostly scales. I've got a lesson plan that my last teacher, Jeffrey Allen, gave me. He wrote a book called *The Secrets Of Singing*, so I just warm up with that whole CD. Then maybe I'll do five songs, some Dio songs or whatever strikes my fancy. Yesterday, I was singing along with Steel Prophet's version of 'The Apparition'. Boy that's a task [laughs].

BILL: Are you a tenor?

BRUCE: Absolutely. I'm actually a counter-tenor, so my voice is naturally very high, much like Rick's is [Rick Mythiasin of Steel Prophet]. But I have a good deal of depth as well, and a lot of range, but I wish I had a little more control. I can legitimately sing within four octaves, but the half-octaves on top and on bottom are pretty shaky. So I have three very strong octaves and one octave of crap that sometimes comes out good.

BILL: Yeah, but then how do you do that live every night?

BRUCE: Well, I like to push myself. I don't like to cut corners, especially doing old Agent Steel songs. That stuff's fucking high, man. Surprisingly enough, it's actually easier to sing than the stuff I wrote for myself.

BILL: How loud do you sing?

BRUCE: Fucking loud. Loud as hell, all throughout the range. Actually, I sing pretty poorly softly. That's one of the things I work on a lot at home. I'm not fond of my voice at a low volume, like when I'm singing to my kid. I feel cheesy when I'm not belting. But I'm trying to find a middle ground. That's one of the things that Harry [Conklin of Jag Panzer] told me. He said, 'You don't have to go 150 per cent all the time. You'll end up hurting yourself. You've got to let the mic do a little bit of the work for you. We are in a metal band – everything's amplified. You've got to let some of the gear give you some help, and that'll save you.' So I try to ease back a bit. I've found that, when I'm really sick and I'm forced to ease back a little bit, I don't sound nearly as bad as I should. When we did *November To Dismember*, I could barely talk, let alone sing. But I used my ventilator thing, a humidifier. That's my Linus blanket.

I also use this stuff I get from Europe called pineal oil. It kind of loosens you up. If you're very sick, it gives you a voice for as long as you're singing. I sang as good as I ever do, but five minutes after I walked off I couldn't talk. But my voice would have lasted for as long as I exercised it. There's another thing called Carvol, although I have not been able to get any of it. They don't sell it in America. It's a caraway-seed extract that's supposed to be very beneficial for your throat. But I'd like to stress that the only time you should do stuff like this is if you have to. It's not good policy to sing when you're not feeling well. It's okay if you've got a cold, but if you've got something more severe, you could do serious damage to your voice. You might not have it for a month.

BILL: What kind of resonation do you feel on the high notes?

BRUCE: If I'm really working out hard, I feel it in the back of my legs. You know how you're supposed to support yourself when you sing? If you're really on and you hit that magic spot, you'll literally feel it in the back of your thighs. It's pretty incredible.

BILL: And that has nothing to do with the volume or the amplification?

BRUCE: I don't know. But a lot of the tones you want to get come from volume. Volume helps certain things, but it destroys things, too. There's a fine line. No extreme, on either end, is going to work for you all the time.

BILL: Being a counter-tenor, growling must not come naturally to you.

BRUCE: It's almost like a different voice, but I can do it.

BILL: You don't have to do that kind of thing very loud, do you?

BRUCE: No, you don't. And I couldn't. Like I said, it's like a different part of the voice, whereas everything above that is very full and natural. In fact, I rarely even go into falsetto to scream. I don't actually break into a falsetto until way up there. It's head voice the whole way. The voice I'm speaking to you with is the voice that does 99 per cent of the work for me.

BILL: So you haven't had any problems with register changes?

BRUCE: No. Maybe a bit, in the past, but I've been doing this for 20 years now.

BILL: So how about the high growling, like Halford?

BRUCE: I don't do that an awful lot because I feel a strain in my voice when I do it.

BILL: Does it hurt your throat?

BRUCE: A little, yeah. Sometimes you get so many different overtones from your voice that you don't need to growl like that. I certainly don't try to keep things ultra-clean all the time, but I also don't try to do Udo either. Like Brian Johnson of AC/DC – he sings with power. He's not feeling any sort of pain or pressure from it, apparently. Like Dan McCafferty from Nazareth, another guy with that same kind of voice who appears to be singing very loud. And his voice just comes out that way. They're lucky to have such distinctive voices.

BILL: Another kind of grit is like David Coverdale or Dio. Are you able to do that kind of thing?

BRUCE: Sure.

BILL: What's the difference in technique?

BRUCE: I guess it's just a little bit more throaty. Rather than relying on my torso to do most of the work, I throw in a little bit more of my throat. There's a tonal thing there. You've got to adjust to catch the tone.

BILL: So you feel it more in the back of your throat?

BRUCE: Just a little tiny bit, yeah. And after years of singing Whitesnake and Scorpions songs, it just etches that effect into your voice. It's a matter of practice. And I'm sure everybody that you've talked to, whether they'll admit it or not, has hurt themselves at one time or another doing this. And youthful enthusiasm will lead to damaging your voice, too. Some people lose it forever. I got lucky because I broke my throat only once.

BILL: What happened?

BRUCE: I felt a click in my throat while I was screaming. It's hard to explain, but I felt a snap right in my oesophagus and I couldn't sing. I could talk, just like I'm talking to you now, but I could not sing for like a month. I just had to rest. Singing was depressing. It wasn't like the depression I felt when I was younger, when I just couldn't do something because I sucked. At least then I felt like I had all of my voice, and I still enjoyed it because I wasn't feeling pain. But when this incident happened, about ten years ago, it was no fun to sing. You just really have to be careful. I'm sure everybody has some experience with that, especially if they are not naturally gifted, and I don't think that most people are. Voice is one of those things where it is not the natural act. There's nothing natural about singing, especially heavy metal. It takes way more work than most voices are born to take.

BILL: What are some of the worst things you think a singer can do for his or her voice?

BRUCE: Sing when you're tired. You need to pay attention to your body. And you just can't get drunk or smoke pot before a show. The embarrassment that you will experience if you take a big dump on-stage is far worse than the best high that you'll ever get. It just would not be worth it. Singing on a full stomach is bad, and here's one reason why: gastric acid. Acid reflux can be really brutal, especially when you're eating a lot of spicy foods. If you find yourself getting a lot of those half-burps that almost turn into a puke, you might want to consider making your diet a little more bland.

And don't over-sing. You may be practising with your band and they may want you to keep singing the same part over and over because they're having a problem, but if you're starting to feel like it's not coming out for you any more, it's time to stop. Your body's going to dictate how much you can handle. That's not to say you shouldn't push yourself acceptably, because otherwise your voice will not grow. It's kind of like body-building – I don't want to make the analogy too direct because you don't want to force anything, but you do need to try things that are not within your range to get into that new area, one note at a time. You're not going to gain an octave in a day. You might gain an octave in three years, you might gain one new note every couple of months – it's a slow process, so you can't do it to the point of pain. When you start feeling pain, it's an indication that something is wrong, and you'd better stop because your voice might break. That's my number-one recommendation.

BILL: That's good advice. What do you do to warm up?

BRUCE: I hum a little bit. If I'm touring, I only do it briefly. Again, I'm really addicted to my humidifier, especially during touring. It just cleans you up, especially if you're in Europe. Everybody smokes there. It tends to tar you up and make you snotty. So I'll do the humidifier, then I'll do a few short scales to make sure my voice is in and locked down. On the road, I don't want to warm up too much because I don't want my voice to be tired. If I'm feeling a great strain on my voice, I won't talk. I'll go 23 hours in a day without saying a thing. I'll write everything. If I'm really angry, I use a lot of exclamation points. At home, I just do that Jeffrey Allen CD. Then I sing to other people's records. If I'm not feeling strong, I start with easy songs before I jump into the hard stuff.

BILL: When you're singing, do you pay attention to your breathing?

BRUCE: Not any more. When I first started, I would breathe like I was singing all the time, right up until the last breath I took before going to sleep. It trained me into always breathing this way, always from the diaphragm. If you watch me talk to you, you'll never see my shoulders go up. I just don't breathe that way. So no, I never think about it. But what I do think about is, I consciously try to remember that even the very high notes are just notes. They're kind of all the same. You can't let high notes psych you out. If you know that something difficult is coming up, you cannot adjust yourself for it. You have to stay doing what you're doing and arrive at that point in the same way that you would arrive anywhere else. You can't gear up for things. Here's a neat trick that Harry [of Jag Panzer] told me about: divert your energy away from your throat. You can hold your mic tighter, kick your foot into the ground or anything, and then your throat is free to react naturally.

BILL: Because the more you think about your throat, the tighter it gets?

BRUCE: Sure. I grab my mic so hard sometimes...it makes a world of difference. It's just something else to distract you. In fact, once you get to a point where you sing pretty well when you're very relaxed, you need to start finding other things to occupy your mind so that you're not thinking about singing all the time. You should do all your thinking about singing when you're practising in your house. You shouldn't be thinking about it when you're on-stage.

Practice is just practice – it's okay to sound bad, because who's going to hear you? Your neighbours? Who fucking cares? It doesn't matter. But if you're worrying about the things you're going to do on-stage, you might need to reassess what you're doing. Maybe you need to find something else to sing. This is a criticism that I've occasionally gotten because I definitely try to stretch things further than they should go. Even if you're doing it okay, sometimes you reach a point where you're really nothing more than annoying to the people. They only have such a threshold for this thing. Often, if you're doing something that sounds pleasant – even if it's not very demanding for you – you're going to get a lot further with your life.

Roy Kahn

Roy sings for German melodic metal band Kamelot, having made his debut with them on their 1998 album *Siege Perilous*. His hypnotic melodies and smooth vocals make him one of today's most captivating vocalists.

BILL: Do you have any special warm-ups you do before a show?

ROY: Obviously it's important to warm up before going on-stage and there are a million ways to do that. Personally, I like being warm in my whole body, normally meaning that I have to do a 15-minute jogging session, some push-ups and so on. It sounds a little strange and probably looks even weirder, but it really helps me. I always start warming up my vocal cords in the lower parts of my range. This gives me a warmer and fuller high range. The most important preparation is probably getting psychologically ready, but that's something everyone who wants to be singer has to work out for themselves. I also drink a lot of tea and water during the day before a show.

BILL: Have you ever hurt your voice by over-singing or singing unsuitable songs?

Roy: No, but I've been pretty sick at times. What I've experienced is that cold or flu normally affects your mind at least as much as it affects your voice. I do not sing when I'm ill, though, unless I have a show.

Bill: Would you provide a brief personal singing history?

Roy: I did not start singing until I was about 18 years old. Some people at school heard me singing in the shower and suggested me for a local punk band. I did three rehearsals with them but found it not challenging or suitable for my voice, so I went to the opposite and started taking lessons in classical singing. I had done this for two to three years, planning on getting into the opera scene in Norway, when I met the guys of Conception, my first 'real' band. I'd always found the form of opera a little stiff and decided to go with the metal dudes. Never regretted that! I released four studio albums with Conception. We split up, so I joined Kamelot in 1998 and have released three studio albums and one live album so far.

Bill: Who has influenced you as a singer?

Roy: My influences as a kid were Elvis Presley, The Beatles, Pink Floyd, The Bee Gees, ABBA and all kinds of jazz and classical. All these were in my parents' collection and thus not something I chose to listen to, but I'm sure they're part of the creation of me as a singer, songwriter and artist. During my teen years, 'Beat It' was my first musical experience that is relatable to metal. I was a fan of the Norwegian pop-trio A-Ha for a while in 1984. I guess it was the shiny vocals and the melancholy that grabbed me. After this, I got into TNT, Maiden and a couple of other metal acts that were big at the time. In 1985, I bought *Rage For Order* by Queensrÿche and was totally sold out on this band up to the point of their million-selling album *Empire*. Today, my influences are life, death, the universe, religion and passion.

Bill: Do you tend to sing loudly or at a conversational volume?

Roy: Depends on the song or part. I'm considered to be a very dynamic singer.

Bill: Does your technique change as you go up the range?

Roy: High, loud notes demand more 'guts', but it's not like a high note has to be loud. I use a combination of head and chest voice in my higher range and at the same time my throat will naturally be more closed.

Bill: Did you always have the range you have now?

ROY: Always had the same.

BILL: How does your technique differ when singing clean to singing with a raspy edge?

ROY: I seldom sing with a raspy voice. Some songs need a raspier edge to them, though, and when I do sing raspy, it's basically by pushing harder.

BILL: How do you improvise when you're having a bad-singing day?

ROY: There is no such thing as a bad-singing day and I improvise all the time, anyway. That means altering the melody line.

BILL: What burns your voice out the most when singing?

ROY: Bad monitoring and thinking about how stupid it was not to warm up!

BILL: What do you do to keep your vocal stamina while touring?

ROY: I don't smoke too much, I don't get drunk, I don't talk loud in crowded bars, I drink a lot of pure water or tea, I sleep a lot and I warm up.

BILL: What are the worst things a singer can do to damage his or her voice?

ROY: That really depends on what kind of voice you have, but for me drinking beer and singing is a somewhat unfortunate combination. So is singing while you have a throat or vocal-cord infection. Cigarettes are one little thing that make life worth living, but they don't make you a better singer.

BILL: What are the best ways for singers to improve their singing abilities?

ROY: Getting into the lyrical concept and singing more often.

BILL: What do you practise on?

ROY: I don't have any specific scales or songs I practise. But whatever you do, sing as much as you can!

Ron Keel

Ron Keel brings new meaning to the phrase 'been there, done that'. He has appeared on 22 releases so far, with numerous projects in heavy-metal and country music, giving him a unique perspective on metal singing. Ron has sold over one million records in his career and has a plethora of videos and world tours under his belt with everyone from Aerosmith to Van Halen. His current band is IronHorse, a maverick brand of 'cowboy metal'.

RON: Upper-body strength, particularly the diaphragm, is imperative. When I started singing, I didn't have a clue what the diaphragm is. Of course, most of us know it's the thick musculature that connects the abdomen to the chest cavity. I've found all sorts of abdominal exercises, especially sit-ups and crunches, to be very effective...but I've also found that singing itself, if you're using the diaphragm correctly, is one hell of an abdominal exercise. Often, after a night of belting it out, the bottom of my rib cage is warm to the touch, almost feverish. Sometimes I'll use ice packs on it.

I have to also stress that so much of singing is mental. It's strange but true: what your mind believes, you can achieve. I've gone on-stage feeling like hell, sick, tired, hoarse...and then, during the verse line of the first song, something happens inside and suddenly you have a killer tone. It's a combination of willpower, focus and training – and, most of all, the desire to sing. That's the bottom line, the reason I'm a vocalist and the reason that I've devoted my life to fronting a band: the desire to sing.

I had two excellent vocal coaches, Sabine in Los Angeles during the early years with Steeler and KEEL, and Sharon Stewart in Phoenix when I was preparing for the Saber Tiger sessions in 1997. I have to give both of them a lot of credit. Much of what I do - exercises, warm-ups, and on-stage and in-studio technique - came from Sabine. Because of her training I've been able to do 200-plus shows a year for the last two decades, a huge number of recording sessions, plus rehearsals, song-writing sessions, yelling at my musicians and doing countless interviews and business calls. The basic premise of Sabine's technique is that the body is a resonating device, much like a speaker, and when all the parts are what we call 'connected', you can hit and hold just about any notes you want to. Tighten up your ass cheeks, tighten up your diaphragm, stand tall with your feet shoulder-length apart, sing out without pushing excess air through your vocal cords. Sabine taught me how to let all the air out of your lungs and still hit and hold the high notes just by resonating the body. The object is to make a clear, metallic tone, almost like a robot. The less air you blow through your pipes, the less wear and tear. Hence the stamina.

Sharon Stewart was almost diametrically opposed to Sabine's technique. Where Sabine is somewhat new age, Sharon teaches by the book, with sheet music and scales and all that. As some people know, I sang metal non-stop from 1980 to 1992 with Lust, Steeler, KEEL, Fair Game, and then in 1992

I went back to my roots and sang country music for five years. I did two country albums and sang in every chicken-wired roadhouse honky-tonk in the Southwest. Then, in '97, I signed on to do an album with the Japanese metal band Saber Tiger, which turned out to be by far the heaviest record of my career. It was time to get back on the metal horse and ride it hard and I hadn't sung like that for five years, so Sharon started working with me on my tone and getting my range back up where it had been during my metal years. Sharon's sheet-music-and-scales technique worked great for that project, because to the producer/guitarist/songwriter Akihito Kinoshita, exact melody and tone were all that mattered; they didn't put a lot of emphasis on lyrics, conviction or emotion like I do. I believe we achieved an incredible balance between the two approaches, and that recording remains one of my all-time favourites.

One of the greatest metal singers ever, Ronnie James Dio, once told me, 'Don't bother warming up. You're just wasting notes.' And when you do this every day and night, year after year, the notes get more and more precious. Luckily, Sabine taught me a couple of invaluable warm-up exercises that get your pipes ready to rock without blowing them out. I start with the 'rattle': get in position with your ass tightly closed, your diaphragm tight, all that, and then put a little pressure on the cords, causing them to rattle. Careful not to push too much air. The object again is to create a metallic, robotic-sounding rattle... This really is a great warm-up. Another one involves opening and closing the cords like you're completely cutting off airflow. Do this three times and on the third time close the throat and suck gently like you can't breathe. These are all I ever do before a show, so I'm not wasting notes.

Recording sessions are a little different because the engineer and/or producer is always going to want you to check mic levels, compression settings, get a headphone mix... The worst thing is to stand there and belt for a half an hour before you actually start tracking. So I go through the vowel sounds, A, E, I, O, U. Starting with A, pick a pitch that is comfortable for you and hold it for about seven seconds. Repeat this once or twice with the same vowel. Then, still using the A sound, hit the same note, hold it for a second, then slide the pitch up five steps or so, then go back down, below the first pitch, all the way down to the bottom of your range and cut it off. Rest a second, take a few breaths and move on to the next vowel sound (make sure you do both long and short versions of the vowels). A lot of people don't realise that the vowels are the only letters in the alphabet that come from the throat; consonants are all generated by the lips and mouth. And some consonants are absolutely deadly: H is the worst. To sing 'Hey!' loudly is to blow air through the cords real hard and that will wear them down. Cheat and sing 'Ay!' and nobody will ever hear the difference.

Some people are just naturally talented singers. I'm not one of them. I've been able to make a life out of singing because of a burning desire to sing and a hard work ethic that enabled me to reach many of my goals in life. It all started when I saw The Beatles on TV in the '60s, and right then and there I knew what I wanted to do, and now I'm 40 and I still feel the same way. I absolutely love to sing. But for a long time I simply wasn't any good at it. I sang along with the radio and records, I sang in my first bands when I was 13, 14. I wrote songs, I did some sessions, I was a pretty good drummer and a pretty good guitar player and I had a PA system and a place we could practise, but I had no vocal talent. I had no clue how to control my tone. I had terrible pitch. I wouldn't have known a harmony if it had bitten me in the ass. I remember playing a party when I was 16; all my friends were there, and many attractive girls my age, and I was the 'lead singer', so definitely I was going to get laid (which is the real reason most of us become the lead singer, anyway). We did the gig and I thought it was great and I was on top of my little world, but after the gig none of the girls would even talk to me. One of my best friends came up to me and said, 'Ronnie, we've been friends a long time. But man, you cannot sing. You suck.'

And then Edward Van Halen came out. Now I HAD to be a lead singer, because I sure wasn't going to play lead guitar any more. So I worked and worked and worked. I learned a bit about tone, pitch and harmony. But two things saved me: I had long hair and I had developed this uncanny high scream from singing along with Judas Priest's *Sad Wings Of Destiny* and *Stained Class*. Now, when I put on my leather pants, shook my long hair around and hit and held one of those high notes, people thought I was an awesome singer. I blew up PA systems and I GOT LAID. But I still was not a good singer. In Nashville, my band Lust took first place in a radio station battle-of-the-bands contest, went in the studio and recorded two songs for a Homegrown album. Both songs became huge hits on Nashville radio. Every time I turned on the radio, there I was. And I sucked. And I vowed that the next time I went in the studio, I was not going to suck.

I found myself immersed in the LA metal scene of the early '80s, fronting Steeler, one of the most popular bands on the circuit, along with Crüe, Ratt, Quiet Riot and so on. The scene was happening and I got a deal with Mike Varney's Shrapnel Records and now it was time to go back in the studio, and I desperately did not want to suck, so I went to Sabine for vocal training. As I mentioned before, her training has been invaluable to me, but it took a while to sink in, and during the Steeler sessions I was experiencing an inner conflict between her teachings and the emotions and style that I was trying to achieve. She wanted me to sing with a clear tone, and I wanted to mix in the growling tone like Brian Johnson from AC/DC, another one of my favourite singers. I was warned that that tone would damage my cords, but I didn't care; I was living for the moment, song by song, gig by gig, and I didn't think I would live to see 40 anyway. The growling tone will take its toll on the strongest of vocal cords, so all you young growling death-metal singers, enjoy yourselves while you can.

I was unhappy with the vocals on the Steeler album. The producer, Mike Varney, gave me four hours to go back in the studio and re-sing the tracks, and I did, but I was still unhappy and suddenly very unsettled. Had I worked so hard, for so long, risen to the top of the LA metal heap, packed the shows and got my first record deal only to find out that I really did suck? It took me almost two years to find out.

In the meantime, the Steeler album became the biggest-selling independent album of all time and it gave me the credibility to put my own band together, call it KEEL and call my own shots. And I still didn't know if I could sing or not. So we were in the studio recording the debut KEEL album, *Lay Down The Law*, and I was producing. We had limited time and budget and we tracked all the music and background vocals first. I think, nearing the end of the sessions, I had completed only one lead vocal I was happy with. On the night before the last day of tracking, I sent all the guys in the band home to LA and it was just me and Mikey Davis, my recording engineer, and I looked at myself in the mirror and said, 'This is it. Put up or shut up.' I went in front of the microphone and never looked back. That was the day it all came together for me: tone, pitch, attitude, conviction, power, range. And, most importantly, confidence. You gotta have confidence, and from then on I never doubted my ability. Sabine teaches that almost everyone is born with the ability to make a high-pitched connected tone, as evidenced by a baby's cry, and the vowel warm-ups I mentioned sound very similar to an infant's wail. After all, most of us are born with pretty much the same tools: vocal cords, mouth, tongue, diaphragm. As we grow up, we're constantly being told, 'Shhhhhh!', to quiet down and speak politely, and we hide our real emotions behind whispers. Two kinds of people never learn: Italians and singers. That's why Italians have some of the most magnificent voices. In fact, the basis for Sabine's technique came from the Italian great Robert Mozzarella. I have spent long periods of time in Italy, and the drummer in my band IronHorse, Gaetano Nicolosi, is Italian. And when he calls, you better hold the phone a foot away from your ear.

Great vocalists often have as many differences as similarities. One is a vegetarian who needs his honey-lemon tea, one has to warm up for an hour, one doesn't warm up at all, some drink alcohol, the others swear off liquor, some smoke and some don't. Some have their various drugs of choice, others would never think of putting chemicals into their bodies. It all depends on the individual, but I do believe that your vocal tone is the sum of many things: talent, confidence, all the mental aspects I talked about, physical conditioning, diet, hydration, what you put into your body and – especially – sleep.

I'm a firm believer that sleep is the number-one healer of the voice. My pre-gig routine includes a nap of at least an hour whenever possible. I don't eat within four hours of show-time; for instance, if I'm scheduled to hit the stage at nine, I'll have my main meal of the day between four and five, an hour nap till half six, then a hot bath. After my bath I'll pop the top on a cold beer while I'm getting dressed and drying my hair and by 7:45 I'm ready to have my first cigarette of the day and arrive at the venue preferably an hour before I'm scheduled to hit the stage. In that hour before show-time I will have a couple more beers, a few more cigarettes and a couple of shots of Jack Daniel's.

About smoking: I smoked when I was a foetus. My mom smoked a pack a day when she was carrying me, my parents were both voracious smokers and I grew up in a cloud of nicotine. I had my first cigarette when I was 12, and instead of coughing my guts out it was like the end of a 12-year nicotine fit. I always wanted to be a singer and during the early years I would quit for months at a time in the hopes that it would help my tone, range and stamina. It didn't. I smoked during all my metal screaming years: right before I hit the stage, during the drum solo and as soon as I got off the stage. I've had an ashtray next to me in every recording session I've ever done.

Then, during the years I was singing country, doing the honky-tonks, I'd sometimes have to do five shows a night, six nights a week. And I believe singing country was even more wear and tear on my voice because I was pushing more air to convey the emotions and I was singing in a lower range much of the time, which caused me to work the throat muscles a lot harder. Once, I had such a six-nighter booked at a place called Toolie's in Phoenix, and I thought, 'Perhaps I'll make it through the week easier if I don't smoke.' So I didn't smoke. Each night I got more and more hoarse, and by the weekend I was barely able to talk. Before the first show that Saturday, I got a pack of Marlboros (my voice is tuned to Marlboros, not lights or menthols but reds – anything else messes with my tone) and sang fine the rest of the gig. I am absolutely not advocating smoking, only being honest about what works for me. I must note that I rarely smoke during the day, and I rarely smoke at all on my days off. I do enjoy my cold beer, but the shots of Jack Daniel's are also usually reserved for before, during and after the show.

When singing rock, I definitely sing louder in the studio than on-stage. During a show, I'm always thinking ahead, to the next line, the next move, letting the show unfold in my head one step ahead of myself. In the studio, all I'm thinking about right now is this verse, this line, this syllable. On-stage you've gotta breathe; in the studio you can pause for a minute to catch your breath, gather your thoughts and focus on the next verse or section. Live, there's no time for that. If I'm doing a live recording, I'll tend to be a little less animated and focus more on the voice, sacrificing a little bit of acrobatics for tone and conviction. When singing country, it was kind of the opposite – I could sing softer in the studio to convey the wider range of emotions, but if I had sung with that much breath on-stage it would have blown my pipes out and I wouldn't have been able to keep up the schedule.

I speak loudly and I speak a lot. Talking softly and whispering is vocal suicide. People often say, 'You don't have to yell at me, I hear you,' but what they don't understand is, I'm just doing what's best for my pipes. I must have some Italian in me.

I know all the tricks when having a bad-singing day. From the vocal standpoint, I revert to the training. Normally it's second nature, but when I'm having difficulty I think about it more, reminding myself to tighten my ass cheeks, tighten my diaphragm, don't push so hard. You don't hold notes as long. You let the mouth do more of the work, over-enunciating and spitting out the consonants. And you have the soundman add some processing – more compression, chorus, reverb, delay. Put a smile on your face, never let the audience know you're having a rough night – get on with the show. I have, of course, experienced burn-out. I have sung pretty much continuously for 26 years and have never cancelled a show because I was sick or hoarse or anything. Looking back, maybe I should've taken a couple of months off here and there to recuperate, but the truth is, I've raised my standards so that even on a bad night I can still deliver the goods.

The three worst things: singing with a headache (I rarely get headaches, but if I do the last thing I want is my own voice rattling my skull); singing with a stomach ache (you can't work the diaphragm so the throat has to overcompensate); singing with a cold (the nasal tone is a dead giveaway that you're under the weather).

In my new project, IronHorse, I have combined my rock and country styles into a hybrid brand of 'cowboy metal'. I have traded the piercing Halford-esque notes for melody. I am now able to sing with more control while moving through more complex melodies. In rock it was mostly minor keys, with the melodies consisting of fewer notes, but now many of my songs are in major keys, and if you saw the melody on sheet music you'd see a lot more squiggly lines on it. In the show, we perform many of the KEEL songs, and while I don't hit the high scream at the beginning of 'The Right To Rock', I sing 'Tears Of Fire' better than I did back when it was a hit. I enjoy the diversity of being able to explore my musical persona in the course of our two-hour show. And it means more to me than ever when someone comes up to me after the gig and uses the words 'beautiful', 'wonderful' and 'awesome' to describe my voice, because for ten years I worked my ass off to learn how to use it, and then for 20 years I've worked my ass off to keep it. And nothing lasts forever, so I'm damn sure going to enjoy it while I can.

Timo Kotipelto

Timo sings for Finnish melodic metal masters Stratovarius, one of Europe's most popular metal bands. He has a soaring, high, clean vocal style that is the perfect complement to the harmonic dual guitarwork of the band.

BILL: How do you manage the register change from chest to head voice?

TIMO: For male singers, you can lower the break. Of course it's still there, but what I do is...with the air pressure...fuck, this is hard to explain. When I slide over this break, what the fuck is actually happening? Let's see...

BILL: It's hard to put into words?

TIMO: Yeah, that's really very difficult. In the past, I read some singing books, and they couldn't even explain it properly. So how the fuck can I tell it?

BILL: Can you explain just the sensations you feel?

TIMO: I think the biggest difference when you go over this break is in the air pressure. For me, it's a little bit easier to sing the notes above middle C and D because you don't need that much air pressure. But when you go down into your chest register, then you need more. The sound comes from your vocal cords, of course, but you have to think of it as coming from your tummy. It should be an open pipe from your diaphragm up to your head. The higher you sing, the more it's vibrating in your head, in the mask, that's for sure. I feel it in the nose and a little bit in the forehead.

BILL: Do you sing raspy in the high notes?

TIMO: Not much. Sometimes I might do a word, but I tend to keep the voice completely clean. That's what I'm aiming for.

BILL: How do you take care of your voice on the road?

TIMO: I try to avoid drinking. Maybe I drink one or two beers after the show, but that's it. I drink a lot of water, and also I take care of my body by doing lots of sports. Sometimes on tour it's not that easy because you have to be on the bus quite a lot. We have a rule that there's no smoking on the bus when I'm there. It's very important to drink lots of water. And, of course, eating is very important for me, meaning that I have to think about the show and when to eat. As you can understand, if your stomach is full of food, you can't sing. That's very important – and to get a lot of carbohydrates, a lot of energy, before the show. If you're lacking energy, it affects your singing as well. So that's also very important. I use a lot of protein, but that's because I lift a lot of weights. Now that I recall, there's another thing I use. It's like salt water that you can buy from the pharmacy. I can't remember the Latin name for it, but this glass pipe is breaking up the salt water and I inhale that through the pipe. It sounds like a coffee machine grinding the beans. It's very good for the voice.

BILL: Have you ever damaged your voice from singing songs unsuited to you?

TIMO: Not in that way, but I've been having some problems when there are a lot of shows and I get a flu. That's a problem. The last problem I had was when we had a festival in Germany almost a year ago. I burnt my left hand with the pyros, so we had to reschedule our South American tour. The schedule was so tight – we had three weeks on the tour and 21 flights, so that was like hell for a singer. I couldn't sleep enough and the air on the plane was very dry, even though I tried to drink a lot. It's cold on the plane, and when you go out it's very hot air. Also, when we were travelling on the bus to the venue, they have the air conditioning on, which is very bad for a singer. So at the end of all this, I had a very bad flu.

We had five more shows to go and I had to see a specialist. I didn't want to cancel more shows, so I sang those last four being very sick. At the end, I had some problems even talking. Singing was a little bit better because you use more air pressure. But I had to take some cortisone to take away the swelling. What happens is the vocal cords become swollen because they are trying to protect the muscles from the infection. Then you can't hit the high notes because they can't vibrate so fast. When you use cortisone, it takes away some of this swelling, but it doesn't take away the infection, so it's dangerous to sing. Probably, if I were some famous opera singer, I wouldn't have been doing this, but we were in Mexico, so I was thinking, 'We don't come here very much, so it's better to try to sing.' So, at the end, when we were flying back to Finland, I couldn't even talk on the plane. I had a note I held up that said, 'Sorry, I can't talk. Throat disorder.'

Somehow, I'm very sensitive to these climate changes. I just spoke to the guitarist for Helloween, and he said that their singer, Andy, had the same fucking problem in South America, so they had to cancel some shows as well. It's very tough touring overseas, especially for the singer.

That's the only problem I've had. One time I had an infection of the epiglottis. That was very bad. I was visiting a friend of mine and suddenly I felt like, 'Fuck, the fever is rising.' I started shaking and I didn't know what the fuck this was. I had some very bad throat pain and this happened only in one or two hours. I tried to drink some water and I had some problems swallowing. I went two days just trying to drink some water.

I actually visited one doctor and he told me, 'Oh, yes, it's all right. Just take some aspirin. You just have some normal infection.' Then I went back home and I was hardly able to speak any more. I couldn't swallow anything, so I had to spit all the slime out. I was like, 'What the fuck is *this*?' Finally I thought, 'I'm not going to take this any more.' I called a throat doctor and tried to whisper to her over the phone: 'I have some problem. I can't talk. I can't breathe.' She told me to go to the emergency clinic. The doctor there told me, 'Okay, we have to take you in now. You have to stay at least some days in the hospital.' Then they had these injections, this liquid food coming into my veins. He said, 'Yeah, if you would have stayed home one or two more days, you probably would be dead.' I'm like 'Yeah...okay.' At the end, you can't eat or drink any more. Because of that disease, which is very rare – I don't know where the fuck I got it – I had to cancel a small tour in Finland.

BILL: Has your range increased over the years?

TIMO: It has increased a little bit. To sing the high notes so they sound not like a mouse, to get the air vibrating in your head, that wasn't so easy in the past, but now that's easier and easier.

BILL: Have you ever had any singing lessons?

TIMO: Yes. One teacher tried to teach me that you should sing with your spine in a straight line, which means, if you're leaning against a wall with your heels and shoulders on the wall and your head on the wall, this would be a perfect singing position. But it wasn't for me. I mean, we are all different, so it didn't work for me.

It doesn't make for a very good show, either – you have to compromise. It's a funny thing that you noticed, because sometimes I laugh at myself when I find myself in a strange position. But it's important to keep your neck in kind of a straight line.

BILL: Do you warm up a lot for a show?

TIMO: I warm up quite a lot. It depends if we have a sound check or not. If we do, then I don't warm up too much. But the guys are lazy, so we don't have them too much. So normally, I start stretching. I roll my shoulders and hands and stretch my neck. If I feel that my face isn't relaxed enough, then I have to massage that as well. There's one secret I have: I'm using a pipe that's made of... It's kind of a silicon but it's elastic. I gargle with that. I have a glass of water and one end is in the water. The other end is in my mouth. Then I make sounds and make the water bubble. What happens is that the water resonates and sends the vibrations back to my vocal cords. It's not bullshit. I go to a throat doctor at least once a year just to check out if everything's okay on my vocal cords and she told me that this is a very good treatment. When some of her patients have vocal problems, she gives them this advice that they should use this thing. I'm using this as a warm-up and you can feel it in your neck. It actually works.

BILL: You just do some scales into it?

TIMO: I just do some things like 'Whooooooo-oooooo-oooooo [owl-like sounds]'. I start very low and widen the range a little bit. Then I even do some high falsetto notes as well. This is only two or three minutes. This can be two, three or maybe even fours hours before show-time. I do it every time. And sometimes I even do it if I have some problems during the show, like if the vocal cords feel tight or I can't keep the voice completely clean or something, then I use this method after the show, but only for one minute. After the pipe, I start doing small exercises very softly. If I can easily hit the high notes, I probably only warm up for ten minutes. But sometimes I warm up for 20 or 30 minutes.

BILL: Do you practise the song you're going to sing, or do you just do scales?

TIMO: Both. Normally, I've been singing the songs so often that I don't feel the need to practise them before the show, but if I'm unfamiliar with the song I might try it out before I go on, but not because of the melody, because of the words – I can't remember the lyrics so well.

BILL: Do you use more power on the high notes?

TIMO: I use a little less volume on the very high notes, compared to the high notes of my chest register, which is the normal tenor range. But if you go over the tenor range – those are the high notes I'm talking about, very high notes – basically that's falsetto. But then again, it's not the normal falsetto because there's a lot of chest register on those notes as well, so I would be singing only using my head and not this chest voice. But when I'm using this open windpipe, you have a lot of air but you don't have to use that much power. Instead, you have to direct your voice a little differently with your tongue. It goes into the areas around the nose and forehead.

BILL: How is metal singing more difficult than other kinds of singing?

TIMO: The biggest difference is that you have to compete with the music. In the studio, it's easier. Whatever you sing, you have to find your own way of singing that song, instead of trying to copy someone else. But metal is more demanding. The conditions might vary from the last night. Today might be a different venue, a different temperature. So it's very difficult.

BILL: Metal singing is aggressive. Is it harder on you than other styles?

TIMO: Yes. Before the show, I feel like I have a lot of energy, but if the show has been good and I've given everything I had, then I feel sometimes very empty and, in a way, sad inside. Especially when I'm backstage and I've enjoyed the show a lot – it's like you have to go back to the reality. I want to still be floating with this feeling like, 'Oh fuck, I'm the king! Ah, great!' It's a strange feeling where it's like, 'Ah, I gave everything', and then there's a let-down.

BILL: The crowd is gone and you're just there.

TIMO: Yeah. It nice to meet a lot of fans after the show, but it's kind of demanding, especially for a singer. There might be people that want to see you, and if you go there, you have to talk a lot. And it's very loud because of the background music and the number of people. Before the show, we sometimes have a press conference. Sometimes I try to avoid them, because of my voice. I love to do them, but it's sometimes too much for the voice. The same with signing sessions in the record stores. If there are a lot of them, I'll only do a few. The fans sometimes don't understand that. The singer's not an asshole; he just wants to take care of his voice. If I had to choose between a nice signing session or nice singing at the show, I'd rather sing.

James Labrie

James is lead vocalist for renowned progressive metal band Dream Theater. If there is one voice that pioneered and defined progressive metal singing, it's James' – operatic and crystal clear.

BILL: Can you tell me a bit about how you got started singing?

JAMES: I was told that when I was around three years old I was already recognizing songs and singing along with them. Then, when I was five, I had a singing teacher in school, and I went into singing contests all the way through elementary school. I would go into other schools and nearby towns to sing in competitions. I started playing drums too when I was five. My dad always sang. He was a barbershop quartet singer. When I was ten years old, he got me into barbershop quartet singing for a couple of years, which I found incredibly invaluable because it really trained my ears. I was really able to key in on notes and intonation while singing with others.

It's kind of ironic because I don't believe that singing in a choir is good for a singer because it kind of masks the individual's voice. You can't really distinguish how well you're singing. If you're driving down the street and singing along to a song, it doesn't sound too bad, right? But turn the radio off and sing that song again *a cappella* and you'll notice that you have to be much more focused on the intonation and the melody. So I haven't been too much of a believer in that. I'm not saying it's a bad thing, but if you're seriously wanting to become a singer, I think the most important is to work on it on your own, and then eventually take some coaching lessons.

So anyway, I did the barbershop for a couple years, and all along this time I'm always into the rock 'n' roll. When I was around 13, I got into bands, doing both drums and lead vocals. Then, when I was 17, I sat down one day and said, 'You know, there's a lot of incredible drummers out there. I have a better chance at making my mark as a vocalist,' because I knew that I was a better singer than I was a drummer. So I started putting all of my concentration into singing.

Then, when I was 20 years old, I started to study opera with a lady by the name of Rosemary Patricia Burns out of Toronto. She taught people such as Yul Brynner, Tony Bennett, Bryan Adams and Corey Hart. She was teaching me the whole Italian approach to operatic singing. It was called 'the mask'. Basically, it's learning how to develop your diaphragm. It was amazing – I'd been seeing her for six months before we even got into the actual singing part. Up until that point, it was all concentration on breathing, tongue placement, lip position, how you raise your notes. Like, you have your lower notes that should be around your chin, then you have your cheek and nose, which would be around your middle notes. Then you'd have what they call the *passaggio*, which is the passageway, which is all your higher notes that you throw up into your forehead. And you need to envision all this happening within. But it's all being projected, sustained and endured through proper breathing and the development of your diaphragm.

I remember doing an exercise she would call 'the alligator'. You know how your chin drops when you talk? Or if you were to yell, I guarantee you that your chin would drop. Well, her method was that your chin stays stationary and you lift your head, almost like an alligator – the top of their mouth opens, the bottom stays and you actually tilt your head back. The advantage of that is that it almost automatically pushes your notes to the top.

We also would do breathing exercises. She would light a candle, and I would have to stand there and take a breath. You know how most people take a breath and you see their chest rise? Well, with this, if you're using your diaphragm properly, your stomach comes out. You try to imagine a big rubber tyre in your abdominal area, and you fill up your air there. Then you would take that and blow the air out of your mouth in a very controlled way. All you could do was just bend the flame on the candle. You would never blow it out. You would see how long you could bend that flame without running out of air. And the key was that you would go for as long as you could. So it would be ten seconds when you first started, then you'd get up to 30 seconds, then a minute. It's all showing you that, if you breathe properly and you develop your diaphragm, you have unlimited amounts of air, which is the key to singing long phrases.

I would always say to her, 'You're my teacher,' and she would say, 'No, I'm your coach. I'm showing you what to do, but then it's up to you.'

BILL: So how long did you study with her?

JAMES: Four and a half years. Then I got busy with touring, so I couldn't see her as much, but I keep in contact with her. A few times a year, I go see her so she can tell me, 'Oh, you're getting lazy there. What the hell's going on?'

One of the key things that she said was, 'If you were to sing at the exact same time every time you sing a particular song, you would never run out of air.' It's like mapping out the song, and it's incredible how it works, but it's harder than it sounds. Some people say, 'Man, that's so mechanical. Just breathe whenever you feel the need.' But if you've taken enough time to prepare yourself to respond in that way, it's not like you have to stay focused on how you're breathing. You can actually enjoy yourself *more* on each and every song. It becomes natural. Sometimes you get caught up with running around on-stage, and the next thing you're holding this note and you go 'Whoa, I can't breathe.'

BILL: Let's talk about the passaggio. Has it improved for you, that transition from chest to head voice?

JAMES: Well, we really worked on that whole transition area. With a lot of people, you can notice the break from chest to head. You have to camouflage it. It was really hard to wrap my head around the envisioning stuff because it's not like an extension of yourself; it's an organic instrument. Nobody can take your fingers and place them on your face in a certain way and say, 'Okay, now that note's automatically gonna happen.'

Also, you learn how to project yourself into the right zones of the mask so that the notes are solid. Up until I saw Rosemary, I was able to sing very high. When I was 16, I was singing Heart's 'Barracuda' and it was no problem for me. But when she heard my range, she goes, 'Yeah, you've got an incredible range for a male, but you're not necessarily doing it right, and it's gonna catch up with you. You're going to grow tired vocally, and then you're gonna get into trouble.' So we had to approach it like 'Forget about everything you've learned up until now, and pretend that you're just starting today.' It was a whole relearning process. But I'd have a gig and I'd totally revert back to my old self because it felt right; it felt comfortable. I would see her once or twice a week, or whenever I could afford it, and she would notice that I was slipping back into my old ways. It took a lot of work, but eventually I would feel it working. Like, when I was doing the hums, she said you should feel the vibrations, so I had to pretend that I had fish lips, push my lips out like I was a big fish. You know, you see some guys going 'Bbbbbbbbbb [flaps his lips while humming]'? In a way, it's the same approach.

And you see people opening their mouths real wide and rubbing their face. And that's great because you don't want to go onstage in 20-below weather and have your face crack. Those are all muscles within your face, so get them loose and everything else is going to follow that much better. And eventually you actually feel the right resonation, and you never feel anything in your throat, which is good because you shouldn't feel anything there.

BILL: When you're on-stage, do you use any resonating sensations to guide you?

JAMES: No. Basically, you're just feeling it. Once you've done it long enough, the paths are there waiting for the notes to come. First of all, it would be really hard to be onstage in a rock 'n' roll band and feel any vibrations, but you can still feel the placement. All I can say is that you're feeling the note in the proper place. To get to that point where it comes naturally is incredibly difficult.

BILL: What do you do to warm up?

JAMES: I do cleft scales, like 'Ah-ah-ah-ah-ahhhh [five-note ascending scale]'. You obviously start at your very low register notes, and you build yourself up gradually. You can take little breaks, have a drink of water, walk around, stretch. Then when you come back from a break, you go into your higher notes. But you never, ever take yourself to your peak – your highest, highest notes. Let the body warm up gradually. Then when you're onstage and you need to go for those extremely high notes, it's gonna be there. But don't be too anxious to get to those notes, and save yourself.

BILL: You're doing it in some adverse environments, too.

JAMES: Yeah. When we're in Europe, the smoke is incredible. You're coughing up phlegm on the tour bus after the show. That's why I also tell singers considering constant touring to drink tons of liquids. Take vitamins like B12 and zinc. I take zinc once a day because it's incredibly good for the voice. It rebuilds the tissues quickly. The B12 gives you energy. On top of that, I drink juice and tons of water all the time. It's hard to eat sensibly when you're on the road, but we have catering, so we can keep it a bit more home-bodied kind of cooking. I try to eat at least two to three hours before a performance, so your diaphragm can expand to its fullest potential. If you eat even an hour and a half before the show, you're pushing it. Then, after the show, you should eat something, even if it's just salad or fruit, to give your body something to rebuild with overnight.

But one of the most important things for a vocalist is tons of sleep. Every vocalist who's out there touring should try to get at least ten hours sleep a night. My opera coach always said that.

BILL: Do you also try to avoid air conditioning?

JAMES: Oh yeah. Absolutely. Air conditioning is so damaging to a singer. If I go into any hotel room that has air conditioning on, I immediately turn it off. If it's a good hotel, you can call the front desk and ask for a humidifier to be put in your room.

Moisture is vital to a singer. You don't want to get your nasal passages and throat dry. That's when you get into sinus infections, which I've had quite a few times on the road. You get worn down, you're under a strenuous schedule, you're going into different time zones and cities – it's just go-go-go. You really have to stay on top of yourself, more so than any other player in the band. A drummer can be out there sick but he can still hit the drums and they'll sound the same. Guitarist, keyboard player – same thing. But a singer, if you have a sinus infection, you can't project those notes with the same tonality. And that's the first thing that people pick up on because that's the most recognizable instrument to human beings, because we use it every day.

BILL: Have you ever damaged your voice?

JAMES: In December of '94, my wife and I went down to Cuba. I got a wicked case of food poisoning, and as I was puking, I ruptured my vocal cords. I saw three throat specialists, and they said the best thing was to take some time off. At that time, Dream Theater was doing the Awake tour, so I wasn't able to rest as much as I would have liked. I ruptured my vocal cords on 29 December and I was in Japan performing on 12 January. It was a nightmare!

BILL: Did you try to adjust the melodies?

JAMES: Oh, absolutely. I had to. But stubborn me, I started going, 'Fuck this! I can do it.' I did it, but I sounded like an adolescent going through fricking puberty. It was very frustrating to me. I was very depressed, very angry. I was going through a lot of shit then. It was a good two years before I felt normal. I had to really watch myself. I couldn't push myself vocally. I still went in and did *A Change Of Seasons*, but I didn't feel like myself until probably '97, at least. The throat specialists said, 'There's nothing we can do. It's not nodes, which we can go in and remove.' I still remember, when I was puking, this note flew out of my mouth that called the dogs. It was so high that it was unreal. Then, ten minutes later, I didn't have a voice. For three days. I was flipping out. I thought that was the end of my career, but thank God I was able to recover from it.

But I'll tell you this: I don't have the extreme high range that I had before that. If you go to the *Awake* album, there's a song on there called 'Innocence Faded'. There's one area in there where I'm singing a high F, almost an octave and a half above middle C, an extremely high note. For me to sing that today... I couldn't do it. I did it then and I could have done it in my sleep. It's a little frustrating. Nowadays I can go up to a D, which is still very high, but not like it was. At least I was lucky after that accident that I could still sing, period. So nowadays I'm quite content singing a high D. A lot of people say, 'I've never been able to sing a high D, so what the hell are you complaining about?'

BILL: Would you consider that as a head voice note or a falsetto?

JAMES: That's head voice. If I went into the falsetto, holy shit, I'm still going way up there. But falsetto isn't real voice. Well, it is your voice, I guess. You can't go up to every male and say, 'Gimme a real high falsetto voice.' They can't. That's why Ian Gillan was one of my favorite vocalists growing up. I couldn't believe the power he had behind his falsetto. It was unreal. We're with the same management, so we've done a lot of shows with Deep Purple. I don't know how old he is now - around 55 - but he still sounds amazing. He doesn't have the range he used to, but he still sounds incredible. His intonation is unbelievable. You should hear this guy live. It's like, 'What the hell? Are you going through a pitch shifter or what?'

Rob Halford, too. He's the greatest. He's frickin' unreal. That's one of the frustrating things for me: I know if I hadn't had that accident, I'd still be wailing up there. But what are you gonna do?

BILL: Maybe there's a reason for it.

JAMES: Maybe, because it gets you more in touch with what's important. I had to look at things in a different perspective, like how fortunate I was. You pull back the reins on thinking you're pretty cool, with a whole new sense of appreciation.

BILL: Who has influenced you as a singer?

JAMES: Well, my all-time favorite is Freddie Mercury. Then Ian Gillan, John Anderson, David Coverdale, Steve Perry, even Nat King Cole. I think he's got an incredibly rich voice. Lou Gramm. Rob Halford. Bono. Steven Tyler. Robert Plant. Tony Harnell from TNT. Steve Walsh. He still has the pipes. He's incredible.

BILL: Do you sing differently in the studio than on stage?

JAMES: No. I approach everything pretty much the same. The only difference is that you're in a more controlled environment; you're much more rested and concentrated because it's the real deal. But you generally take a step back when you're singing live because, if you push yourself too hard, you're not gonna last. There has to be a certain sense of control.

BILL: Let's talk about high notes. Everybody wants to know what the technique is and how it differs from the mid-range notes.

JAMES: Well, once gain, we're starting with the diaphragm. You have to make sure that you have the air. It has to be there. And the muscle development of your diaphragm has to be there, so that it pushes the air properly – not too much, not too little. Then it's up to the vocalist, how much they've achieved that passageway, so that they can not only sustain the note but project it, so that it's ballsy, in your face, and that differs with everyone.

BILL: As far as technique goes, what do you do on the high notes?

JAMES: It's all tongue placement. Your tongue should be as flat as it can. Now, because I'm lazy sometimes, my tongue will stay flat but it will also come out of my mouth a little bit, which would make any opera coach or singer say, 'What the hell's he doing that for?' But still I'm able to achieve the notes I want.

You're probably going to open your mouth more on the high notes. That's why you see a lot of singers onstage who are below the mic looking up to the ceiling. It's almost a natural instinct to think, 'I'm gonna push it up there, so I'm gonna look up there.' As to how comfortable you are, it's a matter of how much you work on it. But I think any vocalist will tell you that there are good days and bad days, no matter how much training you've had.

Jorn Lande

Jorn's versatile voice is a unique blend of David Coverdale, Ronnie James Dio and Lou Gramm. He's fronted renowned acts such as Vagabond, Yngwie Malmsteen and Millenium. He's garnered critical acclaim for his solo album, *Starfire*, and his current band, Ark.

JORN: I started singing when I was four or five years old. My father is a singer and a bass player. He used to live in Spain, and he did well with several bands in the '60s. I used to be on all those tours with my mom, sleeping backstage, sometimes on the stage even, behind the backdrop or behind the bass amp. I grew up with the music. My dad used to bring home albums by Sweet, Uriah Heep, Purple, Zeppelin, Kansas, Steve Winwood, Free, Genesis.

BILL: How about if we get into a little of the technique? How loud do you sing?

JORN: I always try to keep the volume loud. All the time. The music that we do is usually quite powerful. You have heavy guitars and drumming. To be a singer in this you have to try to use that same energy. My energy level starts higher than people would probably think. That's important to me: to give what you've got. It doesn't matter what range you are. If you're low range you've still got to bring power to what you do.

I think I sound louder live than in the studio. That might be because it's chaotic up there, and sometimes very loud, and to hear yourself you push a little extra. And of course there's the enthusiasm of being there and giving it all. In the studio you've got so much for free. It's easy to use a little less energy sometimes to get a little bit more air. You have sensitive microphones; you don't have to give as much and still it's powerful.

BILL: When you go up the range, does your volume increase?

JORN: My high notes are usually louder. I can control them to a certain extent. It depends on if you have the combination of falsetto and full voice. Then you can control the dynamics - screaming loud or, if you want, a little softer. But with the full voice, when you don't mix in the falsetto, and you just use the full power all the time, then it's harder to control. So usually you've got to use everything you've got to do it. That's why people push the mic away sometimes.

I don't like to use too much of the falsetto. It sounds too weak. You've got to bring some of the power. But it depends on what type of music you're writing. If it's something heavy as hell, you just have to make the thin, charred, long note.

BILL: On the high notes, what kind of resonation do you feel?

JORN: Definitely in the head. It's my ears that vibrate. I hear it sometimes too loud. On-stage, I sometimes have to turn the monitors down because I've got to sing very powerful. When they are loud, in the mid range, the monitor starts to crack up and I get this over-steering thing happening. I tell them to take the mid range down because then I can hear myself better.

BILL: Some opera singers have said their high notes feel smaller in the mouth, but in heavy rock I think the notes are bigger in your head. Does it feel smaller to you?

JORN: No. Opera singers don't use the same technique. We use more power. I've done a couple of musicals with guys that sing opera, and when I stand next to them and do the powerful thing, they drown. They're not powerful in the same sense because our decibel level is much more powerful. They have certain notes that they hit that sound powerful and loud, but all in all they always start with less. And classical singers don't usually sing with grit, either, because they have a different technique. The other thing is, they don't use their whole voice. I use the control and technique when I think it's necessary to use it; they use the technique from the beginning.

BILL: When you go into your high notes, do you change your technique at all?

JORN: I have to close more and use more of the muscles in the throat, make it thinner. It's a pipe - the thinner you get it, the smaller the sound. So when you make it smaller, you don't have enough space there to push it from the stomach. You shape the sound and you just push it through that thin pipe. When it's opened up, then you can use the power. You don't have to use your [throat] muscles; you can let it relax. You can let your mouth just hang down.

BILL: To me, you sound a little like Dio and David Coverdale. How do you get that kind of rough edge to your voice?

JORN: I don't know. It's natural for me, actually. But I think it's a combination of how you dare to express yourself. A lot of people teach how to sing in a sense that they can never open up their own voice. They can't sing when things start to fuck up in the throat; they get embarrassed. So it's about breaking that barrier from when you're younger. When you hear the grit, usually people start to choke or they start to cough, and that makes them tighten up more.

That grit is something that you've got to do for a long time to make it actual. I didn't have that grit in the same sense when I was younger. When I wanted some of that grit, I had to force it just to get a little bit of it and used my throat in a certain way to get it. It wasn't comfortable. But then, suddenly, I learned how to use different techniques, so I didn't think about it any more. And now, after many years now, the grit is there.

BILL: What did you do to get it, initially?

JORN: I just tried to rehearse it at around 12 or 13. When I was younger, too. When I was nine years old, I did 'Easy Living' and 'Smoke On The Water' and songs like that, and I had to do stuff like try and tighten my throat to get that effect. But you just listen to music in general and kind of experiment around to find out how they sounded like that. And you found out how they used their breath and how they used their throat and everything. After a few years I didn't think about it anymore. And now it's harder to sing without grit.

BILL: When you were developing your voice, did you ever damage it?

JORN: A couple of times I've done tours where I got a virus on the voice and I shouldn't sing, but I had to fulfil the tour and do it anyway. I almost lost my voice once, but that's many years ago now, like in 1988.

BILL: What are some of the worst things a singer can do to his or her voice?

JORN: One of the worst things is to not get enough sleep. And don't get drunk when you're touring or singing every day. But yes, you need rest if you're going to have the energy to sing. That's the most important thing. Your voice is not an instrument that's made up; it's flesh and blood. You've got to take care of it. Maybe drink some tea. For me, it's been very good with the mint and honey. One more trick is to take hot water and put a couple of Halls' [Mentholyptus] in there just to let it dissolve. I sometimes use that on stage. It doesn't have to be warm. Just bring it on-stage. You can add a little honey to it, too. After a few songs, if you feel like you dry out, a couple of sips on that can give you a little bit more.

BILL: Have you ever taken vocal lessons?

JORN: No. I tried once with this classical singer. She showed me a couple of things, but everything she taught me was just not correct because it's a totally different way of doing it. It's too many boundaries surrounding it. But I picked up some of the breathing techniques, which was good.

BILL: Do you still use those?

JORN: Sometimes. I never think about it, but I think I use them sometimes to be able to control some of the power, to keep longer notes. I can control my air better because I talked to her. But that's it. They always tell you, 'If you sing like this, in another couple of years your voice will be gone.' I just figured I was on the wrong planet right there. It's bullshit. It's obviously damaging to use your voice in a sense that you sing like that, but it's still going to be strong for a long time if you don't stay up all night on coke and drink too much. If you lead a normal life, you're never going to have a problem. Always practise and let it rest for periods, not singing almost at all.

BILL: How about warm-ups? What do you do before a performance?

JORN: I sing parts of what I'm going to sing. Of course, I'm trying first a couple of lower notes to check it, then I increase a little bit and go up in range and do some of the high parts. It's to check it, not necessarily for power, just to feel where I'm at. Every day has a different kind of touch to it. Every day your voice is a little different. Some days, everything is so easy that you don't have to sweat. The next day, you might have to give a lot and you dry out.

BILL: How long do you warm up?

JORN: About ten minutes. That's it. I don't do a lot of scales. Maybe I'm trying to do some half-step notes just to warm up-close notes. I just sing them as ad libs, then I know where I'm at that day, what I have to focus on. If it's harder for me one day, I have to change my way of pushing notes or change from a certain range to another.

BILL: Do you find that air conditioners hurt your voice?

JORN: Yeah. And travelling to different places with different environments.

BILL: Have you ever slept with a humidifier in the room?

JORN: No, I've never tried it. But maybe that would be good.

BILL: How do you improvise on bad days?

JORN: I might change my melodies, make it slightly different.

BILL: How do you manage the register break from chest voice to head voice?

JORN: I just listened to singers. Like, I listened to John Farnham of The Little River Band. He's a Steve Walsh-type singer. He sings always bright and clear but with a little grit, and usually in a higher and thinner expression. I had videos of him, live concerts, and I could see how he pushed and used his body to get to the notes he wanted. And I just figured out that there was a different way of singing. I was used to singing with the full power. So I just learned to use a little less, sing a little thinner, not using the full voice, just by looking at the video and trying it.

Really, though, performance and music should reflect parts of your life. Sometimes you cry, sometimes you're pissed off, sometimes you're scared, sometimes you're a little bit mean, a little bit evil. All the aspects of your life should be reflected in your music. Even though you stand there and do the Dungeons and Dragons and the symbolism about the end of the world and all that, you still have other sides to yourself. Don't limit yourself to be afraid of showing that you can stand there and sing something, crying and hurting, just telling about what's real. That's important. Not many people do that

Tim 'Ripper' Owens

In 1995, Tim Owens was chosen to replace the legendary Rob Halford as lead singer for metal mavericks Judas Priest. Ripper, who has arguably the highest and most powerful range in metal history, is the total package when it comes to singing: blistering high notes, powerful growling, metal attitude and tremendous versatility. Tim was the inspiration behind the motion picture *Rockstar*, about a tribute band singer whose dream comes true when he's picked to sing for his favourite band.

BILL: Tim, who are your major influences as a singer?

RIPPER: There are so many. I'm still influenced by singers. Chris Cornell's influenced me. Ronnie James Dio. Obviously, Halford influenced me. Elvis was probably the first. I still continue to keep my ear and listen and pick up new things, either things I like or things I don't like. I like the raw approach that Godsmack's singer takes. I do like Creed. There is a lot of good stuff out there right now. Union Underground. Stereomud.

BILL: Have you ever had any vocal lessons?

RIPPER: No. Well, I did choir and all that stuff. I had real good choir teachers all through high school who taught me a lot about how to breathe and sing correctly. Once high school was over, I didn't sing in any more choirs.

BILL: In your opinion, how important is breath support?

RIPPER: Breathing is the most important thing in my style of singing. It takes me a while to rehearse for a tour, not so much for stamina but to learn where to breathe and when to breathe – you know, how long I can sing something on a certain breath.

BILL: When you first got into Priest, you were in a tribute band. Was it a tough adjustment to go from singing a few times a week to singing every night and touring the world?

RIPPER: It was an adjustment. I'm in big trouble if my voice is shot now, more than I ever was before, but I take care of myself a lot more than I did in the past. In all my tribute and cover bands, I'd have a blast on-stage – drink beer and have fun. I still wish I could drink on-stage [laughs]. Unfortunately, it's all a business. No more games. I sleep a lot more; I take care of myself.

BILL: There's too much at stake now.

RIPPER: Sure. I want to make sure I can sing as well as I can every night.

BILL: How do you warm up for a show?

RIPPER: I don't overdo it; I just make sure it gets warmed up. I won't sing a scale. It's almost just like a sliding scale – I just slide up from my chest voice into a high falsetto, and I'll do it roughly most of the time. Not super-rough, but almost like a growl.

BILL: And you take it up the range like a siren?

RIPPER: Yeah, I do. I'll just go from low to high. Then I'll start singing a few high notes clean. I just make sure I have my voice, really. I think that's what my warm-ups are for, to make sure I'm not gonna walk on-stage and not be able to hit something. I've warmed myself a little bit more on [the Demolition tour]. I had a really good vocal tour in Europe this time. I sang the best I ever have, so I'm hoping the American leg will be even better. But I'm not too big on warming up.

BILL: So you just want to check the voice to see if it's there. What if it isn't there? Do you start thinking, 'I've got to improvise here'?

RIPPER: Yeah, I do. But the problem is, there isn't much improvising you can do on certain songs, like 'Victim Of Changes', because of the high notes. I lost my voice in one show, and I had to take a few songs out. Out of all the shows I've done, though, that's pretty good. I'm not very good at dodging notes, anyway.

BILL: Is there anything else you do on the road to keep your voice strong, such as using a humidifier?

RIPPER: I don't take a humidifier. I try to swim. I like to hit the steam room. I like to run on the treadmill. Swimming really seems to help me a lot. It's great exercise. I also take licorice root with me. Licorice root is *it!* You can get it in a capsule. I originally took it because a local singer showed it to me. Black licorice is good for your throat. Everybody would know that because it's in cough drops, and Throat Coat Tea is filled with licorice, stuff like that. But I get it now in extract. You can put it in tea, you can do whatever with it. I used to use this throat spray that was good for you. Then I couldn't find it any more, so I decided to make my own. I dropped about four or five drops of licorice root in a little spray bottle and put only a drop of lemon [for taste] because I don't like lemon for my throat. But I would also like to put some Mentholyptus in there if I could get it. So I just sprayed this stuff in my throat, and I actually had it on-stage with me this tour.

I also had ginseng. It's a concentrated licorice-type stuff. It tastes like shit. It's supposed to be like a breath mint, but I think my breath would be awful bad if I used that all the time. But anything that has black licorice is good. And I chew gum as much as I can in rehearsals and stuff.

BILL: Not on-stage though?

RIPPER: Well, sometimes. As a matter of fact, I did all the way up until this tour.

BILL: Did you ever accidentally spit gum on people in the front row?

RIPPER: [laughs] No, I never did. It would fly out and hit my mic, but I'd just suck it back in and chew it. It lubricated my throat a lot. The biggest part is lubricating your vocal cords. That's why drinking a lot of water on-stage is good.

BILL: You do that, too?

RIPPER: Yeah. And I drink a lot of fruit juice - orange juice, grapefruit juice - when I'm on the road, just to get that vitamin C in me.

BILL: You seem pretty health conscious, which is good. So, for you, an important part of keeping the voice in shape is keeping the body in shape?

RIPPER: Well, it helps. My body's not in the best of shape, but I'm probably in better shape when I'm on the road because I'm thinking about it more. But I take care of myself to the level I should. I don't go beyond it.

BILL: Have you ever damaged your voice?

RIPPER: I have a few times, and I probably still will. I had a bad spell once when I lost my high notes. This was years and years ago. I wasn't quite sure what it was from. The voice is a strange instrument – you can just kind of lose it, and you can't figure out why. But I got it back. I've always said that I'm gonna take care of my throat, but I'm not gonna overdo it. If I'm sitting around having some beers and I want to have a cigarette, I will, but as long as it's not when I'm singing, so it doesn't interfere.

BILL: You do smoke, then?

RIPPER: I only smoke when I drink.

BILL: Okay. Everybody wants to know about how to hit high notes. Obviously, you've got a big range. Have you always had it?

RIPPER: Actually, I probably had a higher range at one time, but I also probably didn't have as good lows as I have now, either. But [the high range] was something I was born with, really. I'm a firm believer that it's a thing you're born with. You know, my wife is in the engineering field. She works in CAD engineering. I wish I could have done that, that I was smart in that way. Then I would have been a doctor or lawyer or something. But it wasn't my calling. I was born with a voice. I've trained to become better, but I was mostly born with it. I was always a singer, but when I put on Judas Priest and started singing 'Victim Of Changes' – the high notes – that's when I realised that's the kind of voice I have. That's what brought it out: singing to other stuff. And it was easy. I tried to play guitar and it was hard, but the voice came right out and it was quite easy.

I mean, you can work on it, but it's a natural thing. If somebody doesn't have high notes and they want to get them, it might be quite hard. It's like me learning Spanish all of a sudden. And you know what? Why sing high notes if you don't have them? You can probably put a few in there, but just work on your chest voice and your regular voice. Why try to sing something you don't have? When I sing high notes, that's me. That's what I have. That's why

I made it into Priest. I didn't have to fake it and try to work on singing like Halford. People need to realise that, if you don't have high notes, do your own voice. And work on getting different characters in your voice. The thing about me is that I don't like to sing one way; I like to sing every single way a singer can sing.

BILL: *Demolition* seems to have fewer high notes than the old Priest.

RIPPER: Yeah, it does. It just worked out that way. It wasn't how I planned it. There aren't many high notes in singing nowadays, anyway, and some of Priest's biggest albums didn't have high notes. In fact, *British Steel* didn't have one high note. It might have had one in 'You Don't Have To Be Old To Be Wise', but that's it. 'Living After Midnight' didn't have any high notes. 'Breaking The Law' didn't. Off of *Screaming For Vengeance*, 'You've Got Another Thing Coming' had one, so really Priest still did that in the past. It's just how it works. We had high notes [on *Demolition*] and other notes sounded better. High notes are easy. Any time I did high notes in the studio, I did them in one take. It's a given.

BILL: It's just not challenging, huh?

RIPPER: Well, it's challenging to do it night after night live, sure, but to sing high notes, you're not as particular about them. Just take a good breath, squeeze your balls and sing them.

BILL: Are there any particular sensations you feel on the high notes that tell you you're hitting the notes well?

RIPPER: Well, I just listen to pitch. Sometimes you lose it – you could go flat or sharp from pushing too hard. I'll tell you when I know I have my high notes: I'm a very loud singer, but when I can hold back physically, when I can sing softer and still have the note sound good, that's when I know that my voice is there. I don't have to push it or strain it and I can hold notes longer. On a lot of the long notes, I almost black out. I think it's from a lack of oxygen. You get really dizzy and almost fall over. Sometimes it takes a couple seconds to get your bearings.

BILL: Do you feel any kind of resonation in your head?

RIPPER: No, not really.

BILL: How about the break between chest and head voice? Have you ever had any problems with that?

RIPPER: I always have that break, but it's gotten better now. I can't always slide up from the chest voice to the head voice. I can do it in the studio, but then it's hard to do live on a consistent basis. What happens is that you have to pull the volume down a little bit when you make that transition up. If the beginning note is loud enough, you can power through it. If you start at a real low volume, you can hear the break more. I'm definitely not the master at that. I do it every night in 'Victim Of Changes' – in the slow part there's a little rise after a word.

BILL: Some people say that they kind of squeeze the note a little more as they go through the break.

RIPPER: Yeah, that's exactly what it is.

BILL: Let's talk about growling. You've incorporated a lot of growling into your sound that wasn't present way back on the Winter's Bane album.

RIPPER: No, I didn't do it on the Winter's Bane album, but I was younger then. My voice wasn't developed as much. I've developed a whole other low edge to my voice. At that time, I tried to growl on a lot of songs, but it wasn't there.

BILL: When you joined Priest, you guys detuned a whole step to do the old Priest songs.

RIPPER: What happened was, we did the new album and it was tuned different, so we had a dilemma: 'Are we gonna start changing guitars or what?' So then we decided to see what the songs sounded like when they were tuned different. We thought, 'It might sound heavier. It might sound more modern.' It was a pretty hard transition for me because I sang them the other way all my life. It actually made it harder for me.

BILL: Oh. So it wasn't done to suit your voice?

RIPPER: Oh, no. It just made things easier, instead of [having to change] guitars 30,000 times. It definitely wasn't done for me.

BILL: Are you guys still doing that?

RIPPER: We're still doing that. It makes some songs sound better, but it took a long time to get used to it, even on this last tour. We added 'Heading Out To The Highway' and 'United'. It was hard. I mean, I sat at home and learned them, but I learned them in regular tuning. Then we started rehearsals and it was like, 'Oh, man!' I forgot how weird it was. Here are songs that you used to sing in your falsetto voice or head voice and all of a sudden you had to do it in your normal voice, but *higher* in your normal voice.

BILL: It's actually harder because it's like you have to carry your chest voice up.

RIPPER: Yeah. It *was* harder. Like, on 'Heading Out To The Highway', there's a part in the chorus that normally would be a low falsetto, but now there's no way it could be a low falsetto. But I have a higher natural voice anyway, so I'm kind of lucky.

I'll tell you where we had a problem, though. A couple of songs from the *Jugulator* album ended up being tuned higher in concert. 'Abductors' was like that. We did it in a few shows, and it just tore me up. Like 'Cathedral Spires' - I don't think we could do it tuned up. There's no way in hell I could sing it. That's like going back and playing all the old Priest songs tuned up.

BILL: What's the difference between growling and singing clean?

RIPPER: I just call it singing raspy. It's a heavier way of singing. I mean, Bob Seger sang raspy all his life.

BILL: In terms of how it feels, how do you make it growly instead of clean?

RIPPER: Obviously, you close your throat off a little bit at the back. That's how you get part of the tonal quality. But I don't know exactly what it's doing.

BILL: Do you push the same amount? Do you push more to get the growl?

RIPPER: I would say that I definitely push more.

BILL: Does it ever hurt?

RIPPER: It does for a while, until you get used to it. I had to train my throat to do it.

BILL: So it wasn't totally natural for you?

RIPPER: No, I had to work with it, as with anything. It's just like working out - your muscles are sore until you get used to it. Like today, I got a bunch of shots because I'm going to South America for the tour. My whole damn arm hurts. I got five shots in my arm, man! I swear to God, I can't move my arm. Now, if I continued to get shots, my arm wouldn't hurt. It's like that with singing.

BILL: Let's talk about the movie *Rockstar*. Steelheart is doing the vocals for Donnie Wahlberg in that movie. Did they ever approach you to do that?

RIPPER: No. What happened was, they said they were gonna base the movie on me, but we pulled away from it and they pulled away from it. Supposedly, it has a little bit to do with me, because they got the idea from me, but it's not about me.

BILL: You weren't part of the process?

RIPPER: No. They called and wanted to base it on this *New York Times* article, but they had nothing after that. They didn't want to talk to us. They didn't want us to be involved. They didn't want to know what we were like as people, so we said, 'Listen, you can't do this. We don't want to be involved in this movie. We don't want you guys to say it's about us.'

BILL: So what would you say is the most challenging Judas Priest song for you to sing?

RIPPER: Right now, it's probably 'Machine Man', just because it's so breathy and it moves along pretty fast. But the hardest one to sing is probably 'Painkiller', because it's about the 18th song every night on-stage. I'm so damn tired by then! I would probably do it better earlier.

Sean Peck

Sean is the voice of Cage, San Diego's premier metal band and one of America's hottest new metal acts, currently touring the globe and doing shows with metal legends like Judas Priest and Iron Maiden. Sean has an excellent metal voice with good range and power.

SEAN: I didn't start serious singing until college, until I was 19 or 20. I was like the class clown in school so I was always doing funny voices and mimicking people. I got into heavy metal late, when I was a junior in high school. Musically I was kind of into The Cars, Blondie, The Go-Go's, A Flock Of Seagulls, Duran Duran. And then all of a sudden one day I heard that Ozzy Osbourne song 'You Can't Kill Rock 'n' Roll' and that just struck a chord with me. Then I heard Judas Priest and I really started digging them. So I started imitating all of the vocal seeds of Halford. Then, when I got *The Warning*, I tried some of the Geoff Tate singing. Then some of the Iron Maiden stuff as well. I guess that's pretty good training, starting off trying to sing *Screaming For Vengeance*. You're off to a good start there. But the problem was being able to do that live onstage versus doing it in your room.

BILL: Let's talk a little about volume and range. How loud do you sing?

SEAN: I sing pretty loud. When I first started, the problem was, when I hit my high falsettos, they weren't very loud, although I think that, back in my younger days, my falsetto was more full because I was doing it all the time. I sing mostly in the head voice. I don't use a lot of falsetto any more. The problem with learning to sing and imitating people is it took me a long time to develop my own style. And that's a problem with a lot of the metal you get today. The singers that really stand out to me are the people you recognise as soon as you hear their voice: 'Oh, that's Halford' or 'Oh, that's Udo.' Their voices are completely distinct.

BILL: Do you sing the same on stage as you do in the studio?

SEAN: Sure. But when I record, I usually do one or two lines at a time. Some people go, 'Just sing the whole song three times and we'll piece it together.' I don't like doing that; I like doing one section at a time. That way you can really just concentrate on those exact words and just fully belting out that one section. Especially when you're doing a bunch of different layers as well.

BILL: Do you sing with less power on-stage, to keep your stamina?

SEAN: No. On-stage I give it all I have. In this kind of music, you've got to have the full power or it doesn't have the same effect. And you're trying to compete with a monster drummer and two Marshall stacks.

BILL: Is there anything you did to develop falsetto deliberately?

SEAN: In my old band, Nomad, I did a lot of falsetto. Then, when that band broke up, it was like 1992, and that was the time it was grunge and alternative and no one was going 'Ahhhhhh!' any more, so I completely abandoned all the falsetto for about five years. That was one of the criticisms when I was with Nomad, that there was not enough girth to my voice, so when Cage started I developed a 'Yooowww! [mid-range throaty growl]' to add the beef.

BILL: How'd you develop that?

SEAN: I just kept working on it. Then, in the last two or three years, I've been able to take that same beefiness and go to the upper register, where it almost sounds like a falsetto. And that's where I developed my own style so that I don't really sound like anybody else now. Now, I'm going back full circle, starting to throw the falsetto back in there, which I find is a little bit difficult to do sometimes when you're doing that full head voice growl. Sometimes my vocal cords are just so abused or whatever I just go

'Hhhhhhh [makes a breathy sound]' – nothing comes out. So before I start busting out the meaty head voice, we do some of the songs that have the falsetto earlier in the set. But now I've been trying to work back my falsetto to where I was way back when.

BILL: When you do those beefy high notes, is there any change in technique?

SEAN: Yeah. I feel that you've got to open the mouth a little more and really contract the abdomen. I kind of got that from Elizabeth Sabine. She said that, when you contract your muscles in your abdomen, it creates an electro-magnetic energy, like a speaker in a stereo. But when I hit those high, beefy ones, it's all coming from the throat. And you're just blowing all that power through there. It's rough, man. It's not easy.

BILL: Does it hurt your voice?

SEAN: Sometimes. But like anything, you've gotta just keep at it. When your body is your instrument, you've got to keep it in as good a shape as you can. I notice that, when I'm in the best shape, that's when my voice is going the best. And not just physical condition, but you have to keep practising singing. If I drop off and don't sing for a couple of weeks, I find it hard to get back in the swing. So we practise three or four times a week just to keep it going. When we go into writing sessions, there's a lot of downtime when you're sitting there working on guitar parts and stuff. It's like you work on a guitar part for 30 minutes and they say 'Okay, now sing this part.' You gotta come right in cold and start blasting. So you're in better shape when you're rehearsing the set versus when you're writing.

BILL: What do you do to try to keep in physical shape?

SEAN: Well, I broke my pelvis in a snowboarding accident, so I've got six titanium rods going through me.

BILL: You're a true metal singer!

SEAN: Through and through! When we played the Dynamo Festival in Holland in '99, I was two months off of my surgery. They cut my stomach open, all through the muscles under the diaphragm. The guy said, 'You can't sing for eight weeks.' Two weeks later, I was laying vocal tracks for a demo for *Nuclear Blast*.

BILL: Oh, man. Did you bust any stitches?

SEAN: No, I didn't. And I pulled it off really good. Mind over matter. It's amazing what you can do. It used to be easier to sing at rehearsal than to sing live, but now I find it easier to sing live, just because of that extra adrenaline flow. Sometimes I envy guitarists because they can have pneumonia and still get up there and shred, but with the voice you never know what you're gonna get. Sometimes before a show, I'll be warming up saying, 'God, I'm gonna shred this show. I feel great!' And then you get up there and it's just not happening.

BILL: Is there a difference when you're growling the head voice versus singing it clean?

SEAN: Definitely. I feel my adjustment's in the throat. It's tighter when you hit the clean note. On the growling high notes, I open it up more, just loosen up the throat. If you clench the throat and you're trying to put a growl out, it feels like you're trying to stuff a square peg through a round hole. You have to be as relaxed as you can.

BILL: So what's creating the growl?

SEAN: I don't know. It's hard to explain what's going on, but I feel it in my throat, down by voice box. When I'm doing the higher, clean notes I feel more contraction. I try and relax more when I'm doing the growls. Then I contract the vocal cords real tight on the clean notes.

BILL: That's interesting. Everybody's different. Some singers have told me it's just the opposite, that they constrict more on the growling.

SEAN: Yeah, I can see how they would say that. But I'm talking just about the high-note growling.

BILL: What's the difference in resonation between the clean high notes and the growled ones? Some people feel the clean notes more forward, in the roof of the mouth, and the growling ones in the back of the throat.

SEAN: I think that's probably pretty accurate. I feel it right at the roof of the mouth and the back of the throat, at the top.

BILL: How about warm-ups? What do you do for warm-up?

SEAN: I don't do a lot of warming up. I don't know if that's good or bad. I do some warming up in the bathroom. When I was in the hospital in Reno after my accident, they put me in the shower room. I was still in a wheelchair. I could barely move around, but I wanted to see if I could still sing, so I started belting out some notes, and all the nurses came running in: 'Are you okay? We thought you were dying in here!' But the one that Sabine had me do was where you hit all the vowels, like '[light singing on one continuous pitch] gotta be, gotta be, gotta be...go away, go away, go away...I die, I die, I die...I do, I do, I do...' You go through all the vowels. That was one of the best things I took from her. And she said to do the humming, the 'Bbbbbbbbb [legato, up and down]', flapping your tongue and lips. The tongue, mostly. And then there's humming: 'Hmmm-mmm-mmm' – that's a good warm-up.

But before you go on, you've got to belt out a couple to see where you're at. Normally, I just do a little bit of warm-ups, 10 or 15 minutes, and by the third song my voice is really settled down.

BILL: How soon before the show do you do it?

SEAN: Five or ten minutes at the most. Right before I go on.

BILL: In terms of practice, what do you do?

SEAN: I don't really do any scales or anything. I mean, the songs are so challenging as it is. I just do a little bit of warm-up and then we get into it. And, like I said, throughout the set my voice kind of warms up.

BILL: Do you pay any attention to how you breathe?

SEAN: Yeah. When you get a song mastered, you know when to breathe where, just how to attack certain parts. Like, on this last album, we had to record songs that we never really performed live, so all of a sudden I had to do some of these songs and I could hardly sing them. So I had to really beef up.

BILL: Have you ever hurt your voice?

SEAN: Never permanently. It's weird – one day you're singing great and the next day it's just all scratching. You're like, 'What the hell's going on?' It's touch and go with the singing, especially with this kind of stuff. If you were just singing mellow stuff, it's no problem, but metal is the most challenging stuff. And then we write these songs and I'm like, 'Why did I make this vocal line this difficult?' But it just sounds so cool, you know? You don't want to have to compromise.

I quit smoking, though. That really helped a lot. Now those higher head-voice notes are easier to hit. I'm able to get this upper scream that's the head voice without falsetto. That really opened up a whole new level of power.

BILL: How do you tell the difference between the falsetto and the head voice?

SEAN: I've always had trouble telling the difference. But I think the head voice is what I'm doing when I'm hitting my high, beefy notes.

BILL: That requires more power. The falsetto's more light and floaty.

SEAN: Right. When Halford does his ripping notes, that's falsetto. But it just sounds so killer when he does it. You know when you're listening to singers and you go, 'Is that falsetto or is that head voice?' I've been taking the head voice real high up. It almost sounds like falsetto. And you can feel it in your head. I think that's why they call it head voice, versus your main voice you use for all the verses and everything, which I guess is your chest voice. And the falsetto – I would do these King Diamond impressions, and then, when I would do my falsetto scream, I'm like, 'Oh, that feels completely different.' Like, '[light falsetto like King Diamond] She's wearing white again' – total falsetto, versus the falsetto scream 'Ahhhhhhh [high scream with vibrato, starting quiet and getting louder]'. That's different, and it feels different, but it's basically the same thing. But when I'm going '[light falsetto again] She's wearing white again', it feels like my throat is more open. And it's not as difficult as when I'm really constricting those vocal cords to go 'Ahhhhhhh [high scream]!' Now that's still the *clean* falsetto scream. Then you can throw in the scratchy 'Yaaaaahhhh [gritty high scream]' like Ripper does with his scratchy falsetto notes.

BILL: Yeah. What did you do to get that extra edge? What sensations do you feel?

SEAN: The clean one, you don't feel the pressure as much in the vocal cords. And when you're throwing the scratchy 'Ahhhhhhh [high growl]' you can feel it kind of tearing down in the throat. But nothing as far as the diaphragm. It's the same amount of energy – it's just all in the throat and the vocal cords.

BILL: Hmm. I wonder if your larynx goes up when you do that.

SEAN: 'Yahhhhhhh [high, growling scream]'. I don't know, man. Tough to say [laughs]. When I'm doing the high head voice – 'Yahhhhh [high, growling scream, fuller than the others, with more of a yelling chest-voice sound]' – that's the high head voice. After I do that for six or eight songs, I can't even do the falsetto, because there's so much torque going through those vocal cords. It just comes out 'Hhhhh [breathy hissing sound]' – there's nothing there. But I sacrifice that because I think my head voice sounds better anyway.

BILL: So the clean, high one and the beefy one resonate in different places?

SEAN: Yeah. I feel like your adding more torque to contract it more, so you can push more sound through to make it scratch. There are different falsettos, too. It's just how each person can make them sound. Singing those falsetto Halford notes, I definitely feel it more it the throat.

When we recorded this last record, the producer was like, 'Do a higher one!' Just like 'Ahhhhh [very high whistle-like note]' – super-dolphin notes we call them. It sounded killer. We've got this song called 'Trigger Effect', and I've got five of them in together, and it sounds like one note.

Geoff Tate

Geoff is regarded by many as a living legend in the world of heavy rock. His unique sound, tremendous range, passion and songwriting skills have helped propel Grammy-nominated Queensrÿche to multi-platinum sales, including the 1991 Top Ten single 'Silent Lucidity'.

BILL: Have you ever had any vocal lessons?

GEOFF: Yeah, I've had two separate instances in my life when I've taken some instruction. The first one was in high school, where I had some choir classes and things like that. It really wasn't an in-depth exploration of singing; it was mostly learning terminology and singing with a group. Then, after I got out of high school, I decided I was going to pursue singing as a career. I was noticing that I had a difficult time singing for more than an hour straight – my voice would get real weak and I would lose my voice – so I had heard some great things about a voice teacher in Seattle named Maestro David Kyle. I looked him up and was accepted to take lessons from him. That was very, very helpful because it was a one-on-one teaching situation. I really learned a lot from him. It was a short six-week period, six lessons once a week. He was very expensive and I was very broke at the time. I learned really what I needed to learn and what I wanted to learn. It was very helpful.

BILL: Do you remember what you guys worked on together?

GEOFF: Yeah. He comes from an opera and public-speaking background. He's taught quite a few people who have gone on and done well at their craft. His techniques are really about diaphragm breathing and breath control, opening up your sinuses to find out where your tone is. Probably the biggest adjustment he made for me was that he had a way of teaching young people... I don't know how to express it, really. He helped you find your way. He found a way to instil confidence in you as a student so that you felt... I'm sure that, even if you were not really talented as a singer, that if you stood up in front of a group of people to sing or to speak, you felt the confidence to do that. He had some techniques he shared that really just made you feel like you could do anything once you were in front of a group of people.

BILL: That's really important, especially when you're young.

GEOFF: Yeah, it is. It puts you on the path to discover what you can and can't do.

BILL: So how old were you when you took those lessons?

GEOFF: I think I was 19 or 20.

BILL: How old were you when you got into Queensrÿche?

GEOFF: I was 23 when we got signed. Very young.

BILL: Yes. How do you warm up for a show?

GEOFF: Well, I sort of warm up all day long, really. I warm up in the morning by singing to myself, kind of using the head voice, mostly, just opening up that top end of my voice early on in the day. Then, as the day goes on, I work into the lower registers. Then, by showtime, I'm very warmed up and ready.

BILL: What do you sing?

GEOFF: Oh, I sing the latest material I'm working on, or I sing classical scales, because I'm really into classical music as a disciplinary music to listen to. I don't do any exercises in the vocal area at all.

I really don't think about singing any more. It's become a natural thing for me, like breathing. In fact, I was hesitant to do this interview because I didn't really know what to say. I don't think about that stuff, you know? I think about writing songs and what I want to say with the lyrics. I never think about how I'm gonna sing it; it's always about what I'm going to say.

BILL: Was there ever a time when you *had* to think about that sort of thing?

GEOFF: I thought about it when I was getting lessons. I was trying to put it all into practice, really, which was what my teacher was trying to instil in me, that you just have to make the breathing exercises part of your daily way of breathing, not a specialty thing. Just put them into your daily lifestyle, and that way they become natural. Then, when you're singing, you won't even think about if you're doing it right or wrong - if there is such a thing; I don't really think there is any more. But I think the thing he was trying to teach us was a way of thinking about your instrument at all times, and that practising and discipline make it much easier for you later because you *do* get to a point where it's natural.

BILL: On the road, what do you do to keep your voice strong? There must be certain things that you try not to do, of course.

GEOFF: Yeah, it's mostly things I try not to do. Your body is your instrument, so I try to keep my body strong. I try to stay healthy, get lots of sleep, that kind of thing.

BILL: Do you use a humidifier, avoid air conditioning, use throat sprays, drink tea, things like that?

GEOFF: Oh, yeah, all the time. The air-conditioning thing is really a problem. It's not so bad at the beginning of the tour, but once you get a few months into the tour and you get tired because you've just been singing and singing and singing, then your throat gets a little sensitive. It seems like, in the southern states and the Midwest, where they use a lot of air conditioning everywhere you go, it tends to really irritate singers' throats. Some guys actually lose their voice altogether after sitting in an air-conditioned automobile or building for very long. I've never actually had that happen to me, but I know it gets really, really difficult to speak or to sing after you've been in those kinds of situations. I'm really unpopular with the band or anyone I'm travelling with because I always keep the air conditioner off [laughs]. Everybody's miserable! So I tend to travel by myself nowadays.

The humidifier helps. A great substitute for a humidifier is a shower in your hotel room, running full blast, hot steam coming out everywhere. The whole idea is to keep your body lubricated. You don't need the humidifier so much if you drink tons and tons of water all the time, which I tend to do nowadays because I find that it works better for me [than the humidifier]. If I haven't been taking care of myself or it's at the end of the tour or I've been sick – to avoid all of that, you have to do these things constantly to keep yourself up so you don't miss any shows. You definitely don't want to get sick. So the best thing I've found is... You know those big giant 1.5-litre bottles of water?

BILL: Yeah.

GEOFF: I drink about six or seven of those a day. I always carry one around with me, and that way I stay healthy and my voice stays really lubricated.

BILL: How about cigarette smoke and alcohol? Do they affect your voice?

GEOFF: Well, they say that alcohol affects your pitch, but I'm not so certain that I believe that to be an absolute. A lot of great singers I've heard have a couple drinks before they go on-stage to relax themselves, and I don't hear any pitch problems with them after watching their shows. So I think each case is individual: certain people it affects and certain people it doesn't.

I know a lot of great singers who smoke, so I don't think that's an absolute either, but it definitely deters you from keeping your body healthy, so I suppose it would catch up to you at some point. When you're in your 20s, nothing seems to bother you too much, but if you want a long-term career as a singer, you need to get into a daily exercise program and keep yourself healthy and strong.

BILL: Did you ever smoke?

GEOFF: Yes, I did.

BILL: How long did you smoke?

GEOFF: Oh, longer than I should have. It's certainly not something that's a good thing to do. I definitely don't promote it. The thing that a musician has a hard time with – I know I do – is balancing common sense or staying on a schedule with my creative side, which says, 'Throw caution to the wind. Do whatever you feel like doing and explore the madness of life.' There's always that devil on one shoulder and an angel on the other.

BILL: Have you ever had a time when your voice was damaged?

GEOFF: No, not really. I lost my voice once for a period when I was really ill, and I had to cancel two or three shows. It was awful, the first time in my life I ever had to do that. But that was due to an illness, and when that went away, I could sing again.

BILL: You sing in a clean style. Some singers sing with lots of growl or a gravelly sound, and for some of them it wears them out.

GEOFF: Oh, yeah. Definitely.

BILL: But I think certain voice types are more suited to do that.

GEOFF: Yes. It's truly an individual case-by-case scenario.

BILL: Have you found that your voice isn't really suited for that kind of singing?

GEOFF: I think it's about performing what you feel, you know? I know Brian Johnson pretty well, and we've had a lot of talks about that kind of stuff. That's just the way he perceives it. That's his perception of the way AC/DC should sound; that's the way he expresses himself. And if you have a conversation with him, he sounds just like he sings.

BILL: Oh, so it's natural for him? Do you think that you would be able to do that sort of singing all the time?

GEOFF: I don't think it's a matter of 'would I be able to do it?'; it's 'would I want to?'. I don't think so [laughs].

BILL: Let's get into technique a little bit. Do you tend to sing louder in the high range than in the mid-to-chest notes?

GEOFF: No. I think it just depends on the piece of music. Some things you sing really hard and really push it, other things you sing really soft and hold back to get a little different tone. It just depends on the register you're in. I sing soft and hard in all the registers, so it really depends on the piece of music.

BILL: Have you ever deliberately worked to improve your high notes, or did they develop naturally?

GEOFF: Yeah, I never really think about it. I never think, 'How high can I sing?' or 'How low can I sing?' on a certain part; I just sing what comes out of me.
BILL: It's a great thing that you're able to do that without thinking about it. A lot of people don't have the voice to do it.

GEOFF: Yeah, I guess. But to me, singing is just self-expression. That's strictly what it is. I don't put any other labels on it besides that, really, so it's hard for me to even understand the idea of somebody working on trying to sing higher or sing lower or things like that. It doesn't make sense to me. I can't even relate to it.

BILL: Well, let's look at it like this: if you're going for a high note, are you aware of any change in the way you approach that note, such as pushing more in one area or loosening up in another spot or thinking, 'I've got to give a little more to get this note?'

GEOFF: No, not at all. I simply just visualise it. I don't think in a step-by-step process at all; I'm simply involved in the song and moved by the emotions of the lyric and the music. If the music is really emotional to me, it comes out in a way that's kind of... I like to think of it as not really my design. It's something that just comes out of me on some deep level that I can't really intellectualise on.

BILL: Is visualisation important in your singing?

GEOFF: Yeah. I think that happens through being involved with what's going on, not so much thinking of it as 'Okay, here's the chorus. Gotta get ready for it - tighten up, push, swallow afterwards' [laughs]. I don't follow any procedure like that. Visualisation to me means focusing on what the song is about and what the point is that I'm trying to get across - losing oneself in it, really. That's always, to me, the best kind of performance, either live or on record, the one where you completely immerse yourself in the subject matter and the vibe of the song. Lose yourself in it, and what comes out of you is what you feel. Then, after you get it down on tape, that's when you start intellectualising. You go, 'How did I do that? Can I do that again? Hmm.' And sometimes you can't.

BILL: Does that happen a lot?

GEOFF: Oh, yeah. All the time. When you make records, it definitely does. When you get immersed in the song, you do things that you probably couldn't do, normally. You have to push yourself to that edge. It's like a primitive place in your brain that you go to. It's a way of letting out all the stuff that's inside me. Then you listen to it on tape and go, 'Jesus, that's cool!' And they say, 'Well, can you get one more take on that?' And I go, 'Uh, no, I can't. I don't know how I did it. It just came out.' So then the intellectual process starts, trying to figure out how you did that and then duplicating it. Sometimes I say, 'Ah, it is what it is' and leave it open to interpretation every night if I have to play it live.

BILL: Do you tend to improvise a lot live?

GEOFF: Yeah, I try to. It's all about putting yourself into that place. I'll tell you, live, it's really difficult to do that, for me, because there are so many variables. For example, when you're in the studio, you've got this perfect sound environment and you've got the buzz of creativity going. You're very enthusiastic about the piece of music you've been writing, it sounds perfect in your headphones, and all of a sudden you're going places you never thought you could go.

Live, you're dependent upon the same parameters. You're trying to get the sound perfect, which it hardly ever is. Every night, there's some kind of equipment failure for somebody in the band. Then you have the audience to deal with as well, and some audiences give you an emotional push that's so strong it *does* send you up into that upper stratosphere of performance. Other audiences are like spectator audiences – they might as well be watching a football game on TV. They're just so separated from you, and you can't touch them.

BILL: That's harder to get into.

GEOFF: Yeah, because, as a performer, over the years you develop this performance plateau. I visualise it as a graph where I pretty consistently perform at that level, which is a very high level, but then I have these audiences that are just incredible, that just push you over the edge, and all of a sudden my graph shoots up 50 points. Then I'm in this whole new area where I'm leaping across the stage or singing these incredible melodies that I've never even attempted or visualised before. They're just coming out of me like I sing them all the time. It's intoxicating, man. It's a place you always want to be. It happens maybe once every couple of weeks on the road.

BILL: But when it does happen, I imagine it's enough to keep you going for a while.

GEOFF: It's fantastic! The bad thing about it is, you always crave that feeling again. You're always in search of it.

BILL: How important is physical fitness in keeping your voice strong?

GEOFF: I think it's very important. For me it is, anyway. I think it's probably again a case-by-case scenario. Like, we were just touring with Iron Maiden and Halford last summer, and Rob doesn't do any kind of exercises at all – he's kind of a couch potato – but the guy can sing like it's nobody's business. Bruce and I both run. We're out sweating it off every day, trying to keep in shape, and Rob's walking onstage every night after smoking a cigarette and having a couple drinks, just going, 'Wahhhhhhh [sings high note then laughs].' It's no problem for him.

BILL: Did you guys ever get together and talk about singing?

GEOFF: No, not so much about singing, just mostly complaining about how lousy we felt that day or talking about the stock market or motorcycles, other things besides music.

BILL: Here's yet another technical question. For me, I can tell when a note is shrill or otherwise messed up just by the way it feels in my mouth. The good notes seem to sit on the back of my tongue or resonate throughout my mouth. Do you feel any kind of sensations that go along with hitting a good note?

GEOFF: It's almost like you don't have to hear it; you can feel what the note is. For me, it's more like I can tell if I'm singing on pitch or if I'm a little off by the way it feels. Most of the time, I don't think about that kind of stuff; I just do it. That's because I'm used to my programmes. In the early days, I remember thinking, 'Okay, where's my diaphragm in relation to my throat right now?' and 'How's the note feel in the top of my head?'. That's where I always feel it, in the mask area.

BILL: Right around your nose?

GEOFF: On either side of my nose and right above my eyebrows. If I don't feel it in those spaces, it's usually because I'm singing quieter. Some passages don't require you to belt it out. It's still a point of feeling the pressure there; it's a question of how much pressure.

It's really kind of interesting now. It's been at least ten years since I switched to using those in-ear monitors live. I actually use them in the studio now, too, because I'm so used to them, but getting used to those was a big change for me because it really brought the whole singing experience back to where it should be: in your own personal space. These ear monitors fit right down into your ear canal, so you're hearing and feeling all the sounds of your own body as well as the sound that's coming through your microphone. When you're using regular speaker monitors, you're trying to get them loud enough over the band all the time. You're missing out on the physicality of singing because of the volume of the speakers coming back at you. The speaker pressure is conflicting with your own head pressure and body pressure that you're trying to produce through singing. So with these in-ear monitors, you don't have this conflict. It's a really interesting way to sing. You can do so much more and get so much more detailed in your performance. I really, highly recommend these to everybody.

BILL: Let's talk about the break that exists between the chest voice and head voice. How do you manage that break?

GEOFF: I think the best way to handle it is to avoid it [laughs]. Get out of that area! You really don't need it, you know? But seriously, it's a transition place that's difficult to traverse when you're first learning how to sing, but you just have to keep doing it and just expect that your voice is gonna crack and you're gonna experience some weirdness until you get used to manoeuvring there. You get to a point - at least I have - when you know where the difficult spots are so you know how to approach them. I know I can't approach one area too hard; I know one area I have to hit really hard. You just have to learn where your points of difficulty are and learn how to manoeuvre around them.

BILL: Can you give an example of certain areas that require different approaches?

GEOFF: Hmm, I'm trying to think of what it would be. Doing this interview is kind of good for me, I guess, because it makes me think about all these things [laughs].

BILL: I hope it's not like a baseball player – when you start talking about the swing, all of a sudden they're striking out. You don't want to over-think it, you know.

GEOFF: Yeah, it's like my golf swing. Once you start analysing it... Yeah, I think I'll just be general on it. It's just a matter of practice and experimenting with the voice pressure. Certain areas of certain registers you have to hit hard, others you have to hit softer.

BILL: Who's influenced you and inspired you as a singer?

GEOFF: Probably my biggest influence in my early years, when I was discovering what I could do with my voice, was Ann Wilson from Heart. I used to sing along with her records and I found that I could do most of the things she could do. I went, 'Oh, this is kinda cool, a man singing that high.' Then I started playing around with stuff that Bowie did in his lower area. Bowie can sing kind of high, too. So I'd say Bowie and Ann Wilson, really. I think Ann Wilson is probably the best female rock singer ever. She was just fantastic.

BILL: How important is breathing technique?

GEOFF: When you're first learning, I think breathing technique is incredibly important to master. It's definitely what saves you in the endurance area of singing. It's what makes it so you can sing those two-hour shows. It's like any instrument – you've got to practise it to get good. I think so many people get frustrated and give up, or they learn how to do it in a different way that doesn't require so much discipline. And you hear it all over, like in today's pop music – you hear all these young kids singing who really can't sing well at all. They're relying heavily on the technological gizmos that we've created, auto-tunes and auto-pitches and things like that. These things sort of mask the inadequacies, and they do a really good job, but you can definitely tell the difference live. I guess, if you're not a good player, you can seem very good on record, but the real test is live. How can you pull it off live?

BILL: Pavarotti said in an interview that, when he sings, the breath-support muscles operate like you're going to the bathroom, like a big bowel movement.

GEOFF: Yeah. It's also like doing squats in the gym. In fact, you'll notice that really good singers don't have the six-pack abs. You can't develop those particular ab muscles extensively if you're a singer because it reduces your diaphragm abilities. Most singers are more barrel-chested.

Joe Lynn Turner

The musical career of Joe Lynn Turner has spanned over 25 years and he has sung for renowned acts such as Deep Purple, Yngwie Malmsteen, Fandango and Rainbow, for whom he sang their 1983 Number One hit 'Street Of Dreams'. He has a versatile voice that can be heard on albums with rock greats like Billy Joel, Lita Ford, Michael Bolton and Cher. He has recorded nine solo albums and continues to forge a successful solo career.

BILL: Joe, can you give a brief history of when you started singing?

JLT: When I was young, I used to listen to all the Motown records and AM radio, which was at that point commercial pop music. My parents tell me I would hum a tune, but it was nothing serious. Basically, all this really started when my pop got me playing accordion when I was, like, ten years old. It was a terribly unsexy instrument, so he brought home a guitar that he was learning to play and some Elvis Presley books to learn from, and I picked up his guitar and started playing 'Love Me Tender' and whatnot. Then The Beatles came out and that was it, that was the end of the beginning. I said, 'I've gotta have this.' I mean, all the chicks were after the guys in the bands; it's been the same old story since day one for everyone. That's why 90 per cent of the people get in this business, because a) we're insecure and we need it - we need the attention - and b) we probably have something to say, some kind of passion inside us that needs to come out. So, with these two factors, I started playing guitar, and I sang a Beatles song that made this girl down the block go crazy with emotion; she started crying, and I went, 'That's it! I'm doing this!' I couldn't get a turn before that - nobody would even look at me - so it was one of these things where this little nerd turns into this guy who can sing.

BILL: And it just so happened that you were a hell of a singer?

JLT: No, honestly! I started singing because the singer in our band - we had a band called The Other Side, and we were playing school dances - he got sick. He started throwing up and everything. There we were at the dance and we had to finish the set. I was singing backing and playing lead guitar, so I was the only other person who could do this, so I started singing all the Doors and Deep Purple songs that we were covering and more and more people started to come up front, so I started to realise, 'They must like my voice.' Then I got a lot of accolades about it, so the singer was out and I was in. That's how I started singing lead. It was an accident, really.

BILL: So who or what influenced you as a singer?

JLT: Everything from the pop, melodic stuff to the Motown soul stuff. I used to sing a cappella with a lot of black friends. We'd go in the park, man, and these guys were older, so they'd drink their wine and I'd sing all the high parts because I was just a little kid. They said, 'Man, you've got soul,' and I started to believe it. I was like, 'Cool!' I listened to Otis Redding, Sam Cooke and Wilson Pickett. There weren't too many white singers I couldn't copy. I mean, back in those days it was Garry Puckett And The Union Gap, so that was pretty easy. And Neil Diamond - pretty easy. It was the black singers who I really went after. I thought James Brown and all these cats were just the baddest cats. Plus I like Stevie Wonder. So I used to go to the Apollo with my black friends, and I was the only white kid there. Otis Redding would be singing 'Try A Little Tenderness', and that would be it for me. And I still imitate him to this day. It's crazy.

BILL: Well, he's a good singer.

JLT: Great singer, man!

BILL: I liked Three Dog Night's version of that song, too.

JLT: Oh, now there was another band that really had soul! We would actually do a lot of Three Dog Night songs with three- and four-part harmonies.

BILL: Have you ever taken any lessons?

JLT: Yeah. If you're gonna build a house, you've gotta get a hammer. When Fandango was going for a record contract, my father said, 'Man, you'd better get some lessons,' and I said, 'You're right, because this is gonna be professional now.' I tried out a whole bunch of different teachers. You really have to get along with them and communicate deeply with them. So, if you don't, you've got to move on to the next. I moved along until I finally found this one guy - not by accident, either -

this guy by the name of Martin Lawrence. I know it sounds like the comedian, but...

BILL: Not him?

JLT: Absolutely not him. Basically, he said, 'Look, I can't teach you how to sing,' and I looked at him – like, 'Well, you're a voice teacher, aren't you?' He said, 'Yeah, I'll teach you how to hit the notes, but as far as singing goes, it's all soul, and that's a gift from God.' And I knew what he meant, because all the singers that I was imitating had it, and I could tell when someone could really sing and when someone could just hum a tune. There's a big difference in really hearing that extra gift come across. That's what separates the men from the boys. So I was lucky enough to be somewhat gifted.

All we did was singing exercises. Never once did Marty hear me sing a song, except on the CDs. He'd say, 'Nice. Great. Beautiful emotion here – wonderful. You made a tear come out of my eye.' But we worked on technique, because you can't teach soul, man.

Marty taught me that singing is very mental, although it's very physically demanding, probably as demanding as the drummer's job. I played guitar, man, and you could do that hungover, but you can't sing like that. I think singing and drumming are the most physically demanding gigs on-stage. Guitar players can be skinny little drunks, fine, but to sing you've got to be in some kind of shape.

So Marty taught me that singing is a mental thing. You have to place the note. You've got to think of that note before it happens – the phrasing and everything. That's a technique that develops through experience, I think. The mental part of it was really new to me because I didn't think of it that way. Marty taught me that singing is like a pyramid – the high notes are smaller and pointed and the low notes are wider. He also taught me about using the cover tones, which is really important. Instead of hitting a really hard 'Eee', you hit an 'Eh' and it will still sound like an 'Eee'. But if you widen your mouth to hit an 'Eee', you screw up your vocal cords. So you have to keep your mouth in an oval shape, almost like a choirboy. And it works.

BILL: Let's talk about volume a little bit.

JLT: Well, unfortunately, I'm not as gifted as some, so I'm an extremely loud singer. I don't really have a falsetto – I use chest and head voice and that's it. Falsetto I was not gifted with, and I'm very envious because it's such a remarkable tool when needed. But you learn to work with what you have. Marty taught me how to hit some seriously high notes. For example, I couldn't sing over an A-440 [440Hz – middle A] when I went to him, and now I can hit above a high E, which is nuts. That's metal screaming. This technique took my range up another octave and a half.

BILL: What technique is that?

JLT: It's like stretching a rubber band up and down at the same time. Marty taught me how to fill up the diaphragm – not the lungs; [expanding the abdomen, not the chest]. While you keep the air trapped there, you let all the air out of your lungs, [exhaling in a way that deflates the chest while keeping the breath-support muscles in the abdomen distended]. Most people think they have to take big breaths, but it's not about big breaths; it's really about holding the air inside the solar plexus. This is why a lot of big singers have barrel chests, because of this muscle development. For a small guy, I have this huge chest because of these muscles in the solar-plexus area.

What you do is you hear the note before you sing it, and all at the same time you push down with the bottom half of your body, and that means you push down your guts. It's like going to the bathroom. You push down that way and pull up the other way – like a rubber band – to hit the high note. You pull the high note up while you're pushing down.

BILL: You feel the resonations in different spots, obviously, for different notes.

JLT: Absolutely. Like, on this last record, in the studio I have to take Advils before I sing because I'll definitely get a headache. There's no question about it. I will sing so hard and so high and with such passion that I will be straining my whole body. It's kind of like lifting weights – you're gonna feel it afterwards.

I know singers who are too delicate. I told this one guy, a very famous singer (but I won't mention any names), 'You've got to get away from this pampering yourself like some diva. Grab a bottle of Jack Daniel's, smoke a cigarette, kiss a girl. Do something that's gonna bring your singing ability from your heart and your soul, as opposed to worrying about what you're doing with your throat.' And this guy's got a five-octave range – he's incredible. He beats the shit out of me, as far as range is concerned, but he's mentally locked up. And a lot of guys will do that.

But singers struggle with this every day. You wake up and go, 'Can I still do it?' The problem is, people sing out of their own keys. Not everybody can do everything – except Glenn Hughes; he can do everything. He's just got this huge range. It's sick. Glenn has a sweet tone as well as the hard tone, and make no mistake, there's a big difference with singers that can sing hard and soft. He can tear your heart out on a ballad and then rip it up on a rock song. Now, Dio has never done a ballad in his entire life. He just doesn't have the voice for it. And why put yourself in a situation that's going to embarrass yourself? I mean, I wrote a song this time that was out of my range and didn't make the record. I actually *wrote* it out of my range. So we'll record it for the next album and put it in a proper key. But I was singing an octave lower, and I went, 'I'm never gonna make this.' Some of the tones are gnarly up there for me, they're kind of ratty, so I don't like that.

BILL: It's important to know your voice.

JLT: Yeah, and it's important to be proud of what you have, and also to know your limitations. Make the best out of what you've got. Soul is what I look for in a singer. I mean, range is impressive, and all that kind of stuff, but that's all technical. Take Bruce Springsteen, who's got a one-octave range – he can emote something in a lyric that will knock your socks off. My dad used to sing with Frank Sinatra, and Frank was never a great singer. Frank's delivery was what it was all about. Delivery of the lyric is so important.

BILL: When you're on the road, what do you do to keep your voice in shape? Some guys try to avoid air conditioning or use a humidifier.

JLT: That's true. The air conditioning screws with your voice. The other thing is, sometimes the room will have this forced, hot-air heat. You'd better put a bowl of water out, fill your bathtub up or carry a humidifier. On tour sometimes, I have a humidifier with me – my room's, like, soaking wet, the walls are dripping. You've gotta keep the voice moist. Now I bought this little humidifier no bigger than a cell phone. It has a cup that goes around your nose and your mouth. I just breathe in and out to wet the voice and loosen the sinuses. Usually I'll do that before a show for a good half-hour. Sometimes, during a drum solo or something, I'll run backstage and take a couple of shots of that.

And you've gotta drink a lot of water. I've done enough drugs and drink to know that both of those will drain the life out of your organs. Alcohol is a drying agent. Just put rubbing alcohol on your skin and see what it does. Now, if you drink it, what the hell do you think it's doing to your insides?

BILL: What else do you do on the road to keep your voice in shape?

JLT: The main thing is that you try to get sleep. That's the most difficult thing on the road. For a singer, it's like, if you had a pea under your mattress last night, you felt it. It's hard to get to sleep right after a show. It takes time to wind down. Plus, you have to take a quick shower because you don't want to be stinking and sweaty and salty. Next thing you know, you get into a thing where you're taking Excedrin PM to get to sleep because it's 1am and you have to be in the lobby at 5am to get on another plane to go do another show that day.

But once you get through that first month or so on the tour, you're like iron; you can withstand it. I warm up before every show, just doing some scales. And you have to support the notes. If you don't, the cords are going to take the abuse.

BILL: You don't feel any tension in your throat when you're singing, do you?

JLT: I try not to. If I do feel tension, I try to completely relax. Jimi Jamison from Survivor told me, 'You just go out there and go easy. Let the mic do the work.' He's so right. You've got to just ease into it.

Now, after you get going, you can enter a zone where you're really drawing power from a higher source. I know I experience it, Glenn Hughes has experienced it and everyone who I admire, that I've talked to, experiences it. You literally touch the hand of God sometimes. When you're on, it's just unbelievable. I've always said that I don't sing. He sings. I'm just a vehicle.